BRONX TO BROADWAY

A Life in Show Business

Harold Thau

with
Arthur Tobier

Bronx to Broadway: A Life in Show Business
By Harold Thau with Arthur Tobier
Copyright © 2002 by Harold Thau
ISBN# 1-55783560-8

Library of Congress Cataloging-in-Publication Data: 2001012345

TK

**APPLAUSE THEATRE &
CINEMA BOOKS**
151 W46th Street, 8th Floor
New York, NY 10036
Phone: (212) 575-9265
Fax: (646) 562-5852
email: info@applausepub.com
www.applausepub.com

COMBINED BOOK SERVICES
LTD.
Units I/K, Paddock Wood
Distribution Centre
Paddock Wood, Tonbridge,
Kent TN 12 6UU
Phone: (44) 01892 837171
Fax: (44) 01892 837272

SALES & DISTRIBUTION, HAL LEONARD CORP.
7777 West Bluemound Road, P.O. Box 13819
Milwaukee, WI 53213
Phone: (414) 774-3630 Fax: (414) 774-3259
email:halinfo@halleonard.com
internet: www.halleonard.com

BRONX TO BROADWAY

A Life in Show Business

Harold Thau

with
Arthur Tobier

APPLAUSE
THEATRE & CINEMA BOOKS

ACKNOWLEDGMENTS

I would like to express thanks to the following people who helped in one way or another with the process of recollecting the stories embodied here:

To Dorothy, my partner and soul mate, who has inspired me through thick and thin, and with whom I've lived this life in show business.

To my children, Michael and Amy, wunderkinds and humanists; my pride in them is ongoing.

To the four people who have meant so much to me professionally: Steve Burn, my business partner for 30 years, my confidant, and one of the smartest businessmen I know; Milt Okun, who has taught me much of what I l know about music and who has always been there for me; John Denver, the brother I never had and always longed for: a genius in his craft, a true American hero; and John Malkovich, my friend, whose talent and integrity has always been an inspiration to me.

To Joan Candee, my associate, who I have laughed with, and with whom I have fought the battles side by side.

Last and not least to Arthur Tobier, collaborator and friend, who brought patience, experience and insight to the editorial task.

The Pantheon

"As a child, you accept the manmade background itself as the inevitable nature of things; you don't realize that somebody once drew lines on a piece of paper who might have drawn otherwise."

The plane is circling the Apple, and I'm straining to look through a port-hole to see if I can spot the place where old times had been called simply yesterday, today and tomorrow. The woman, over whose lap I'm hover-ing—it's the young Simone Signoret from "A Room at the Top," asleep until that moment—asks with that droll assurance only movie stars have, 'Why so curious?'

'What do you see down there that doesn't go on everywhere?

The plane banks left, tilting our side upward so that in the glare of the late summer sun everything turns white for a second.

"Old times," I say.

"Old times?" she responds, puzzled by the expression.

"The past," I say. "My past."

"Down there? Mais non! Down there is nothing but the present," she says emphatically.

Again the plane banks, to the right this time, and we both look. Simone

1

sees nothing that means anything to her. I spot the unmistakable mass of the tower of my junior high school. When it opened in 1929 (just ahead of the Crash), it caused a stir among the cognoscente. Architecturally and pedagogically, inside and out, the school was seen (by who exactly I don't know) as a 'herald of a new age' in educating us would-be parvenues. Unfortunately the shiny optimism didn't last into our time. We got the physical embodiment of the new age but the philosophy got eaten up by the Depression. On the other hand, it was where I copped my first 'feel' (on a crowded staircase, a moment of tenderness beyond mothercare: I thought love would follow), and then saw 'theater,' maybe for the first time, a high school troupe doing Odets: "Awake and Sing." It was us!

Only we were the class of 1949...

"In France," Simone says, "we separate the past from the present."

"How so? How do you do that?

"We have the Pantheon. Do you know it?"

"The Pantheon? Of course, the palace of the greats."

"Yes, the Pantheon is where we place our heroes."

"Heroes?"

"Yes, those who embody our past."

"I see, " I say, still straining to catch a glimpse of something recognizable in the patchwork of streets down below.

"You don't look convinced."

"It's not that, really. I just wasn't thinking of the past in those terms. What I was thinking of had personal meaning. But a pantheon isn't a bad idea."

The plane banks again and the Bronx streets below, a crazy quilt of intersecting lines, come up at us. I pick up the Boston Post Road where it separates itself from Third Avenue–which I could identify by the bridge to the south of it, and follow the road north past where I used to live, all in an instant. In his presidency, Jimmy Carter had visited those streets and had had them declared a disaster area, a symbol of urban decay–there where I used to meet my father coming home from work and where, precociously, I had shaped an entrepreneurial imagination. "Had it all sim-

ply vanished," I wondered, squinting to take in the details of the streets below? "Even the way the boys there grew up?"

From our great height, we kept circling the city.

"A pantheon isn't a bad idea," I heard myself saying again.

With the provision of a cheap rapid transit system from lower Broadway out to New York City's hinterlands at the turn of the century, the Bronx underwent intense development; especially in Morrisania, where my folks went to live in the early Thirties. By the time my friends and I came on the scene looking for action, the place had long been transformed, and it all seemed natural to us.

1

Last of the New York Indians

Before we knew how we wanted to live, even before anything remotely approaching direction or purpose, or understanding of where in the greater scheme of things we belonged and how it mattered; before the Superbowl, three-point plays, designated hitters, instant replay; before either corporate America or Aquarian Age metaphysics took hold; before Elvis, Clinton, Bush, Carter, Reagan, Ford, Nixon, Kennedy and Eisenhower, there was just us: this group of pint-sized public school boys by day, learning the basics of the American credo as FDR's New Deal defined it, and the last of the New York Indians (as my mother would call us) by night , standing obscurely at a corner of a crossroads in the East Bronx, like birds on a wire.

But our obscurity didn't recognize itself as that. Our obscurity had its own culture, its own ordering of knowledge, its own perfect moments, even a history; for even obscurity has texture. Obscurity for us was not just 'a stage in the ongoing national drama,' as the historians were apt to portray it, but in the local context it was a staging ground for intricate deal-making, and a viable launching pad for 'easy street.' We were collectors of American experience in pursuit of a dream.

Standing on the corner, we wrapped the night around us, shifted in our places like the old men, and waited; innocence personified. Between us there was little guile, as I think of guile these days. There was even less by way of preconception. We took in whatever there was to see as though the world beyond would simply reveal itself if

we looked at it long enough. Close at hand, prodded by circumstances, were all the dichotomies any of us needed to learn the great
lessons about good and evil, right and wrong, rich and poor, black
and white. Whenever weather allowed, generations gathered there,
on that corner: fathers and sons mostly, like some Carpathian strong-
hold, listening to and telling the up-to-the-minute stories. Talking
and taking in the voices.

The talk, I think, made us all feel part of the flow of the time we
were in, although as I remember it we had not the foggiest notion of
it being a particular time, standing there, just after the Second World
War, in front of Gittelson's kosher delicatessen and Sam's candy
store, two of the entrepreneurial giants of our part of the United
States, at a point on Boston Road from where you could see and hear
the uptown and downtown Bronx Express rumbling by, not that far
overhead, on the elevated tracks above Southern Boulevard a block
away. Time for us began that morning, with the pressing events of
the day.

Our schemes were seldom of consequence: consequence, impact,
profundity were not the issues. In fact, being sealed off from consequence seemed like the thing to be. Not so far off that we couldn't

 imagine it, people
our parents knew
were caught in the
maelstrom of a
war; so we did
well to be obscure,
out of harm's way.
What was impor-
tant to us, in all
the talking, was

just being there, doing it. If we talked long enough, we figured,
inspiration would arrive, and carry us off on some great adventure:
to the Grand Concourse, to the Bronx Zoo, to Madison Square
Garden, downtown to Broadway.

What bound us, spiritually and culturally, was that we were all there, in our obscurity, on the same level. That fact; possibly the place in our psyches of the 10 Commandments, which we had all, or mostly all, nailed down in Hebrew School, memorized if not internalized; and, lastly, the shared memory of that magnificent morning one gray Saturday, in the fall of 1944, when we got a glimpse of FDR, our leader in the flesh, driving through in an open car on what would be his last presidential campaign. Pale and wan, and waving to us, he was already a dying man. But for a moment the bubble of our obscurity was pierced. That hand

FDR's last hurrah, October 1944. He drove through the Bronx, and then downtown to Broadway to a rally in the garment district.

waving in our direction was the laying on of recognition for our collective aspiration to be citizens of a world larger than the one we knew there.

No one yet recognized that we were standing at the edge of the outermost limit of an expanding universe, that light and time would soon collide and carry us off in unsuspected directions, and that everything in our universe that we considered solid would disappear from the place, along with us. Our family stories had different histories to enact, and through them we had different dreams to apprehend. Not to mention the unexplored libidos. Yet there, under that one Bronx sky, we jelled; in our sense of democratic possibilities, we defined each other. It is said now that we're not a melting pot, but some other kind of amalgam, which may be so. But during the war and its aftermath, in that place, I think we were that melting pot.

It still shows up for me that way. I still hear the presumptive tongue that we contrived for ourselves, along with all the other New York Indians in the city during that same period; it shows up in the most unlikely places. It showed up encoded in an invitation that reached me in London one foggy English evening. Dorothy read the invitation to me over the phone:

> Dear 173rd Street, Minford Place, Crotona Park, Mohawk and Marvels Alumni and wives or girlfriends:
> The Gala Reunion has been organized, reorganized, and modified, and is now ready to take place.
>> Date: Saturday Night, October 18, 1980
>> Time: 8 PM
>> Place: Holiday Inn, Yonkers, New York
>> Price: $40 per couple ($20 single)
> Our treasurer promised he won't abscond with the funds, and the other members of the Committee have guaranteed constant surveillance.
> This reunion promises to be the best, with ample time for eating, drinking and catching up on old times.

There had been so much in the news about the demise of the South Bronx. The stories I read had nagged at me; the place itself was made the villain. I knew it as a place of endless possibilities. As Dorothy read, part of me, in deep remission, was jolted awake.

I had been a couple of weeks on the road doing business: John Denver, whose interests I managed, was closing a tour at the Royal Albert Hall, and enjoying incredible success as a performer. I'd come to London to see the performance. Also I'd been going through the life-altering process of producing a new play in a little theater in the West End of London. I was in another realm literally and metaphorically.

But there in the jaunty cadences of that simple note, I could hear the clarion call. I recognized the voice of the Jewish Bronx in its state of amused self-mockery. 'Old times' were the furthest thing from my mind, but on the flight home phantom shapes started to materialize. Midway over the Atlantic, my fatigue brought on a deep sleep, and I dreamed of reunion.

The plane is circling the Apple, and I'm straining to look through a porthole to see if I can spot the place where old times had been called sim-

Hermann Ridder Jr. High School, an art deco masterpiece built in 1929 that tried to varnish us over with a layer of formal learning, and the street corner, in front of Gittelson's delicatessen (in the lower right-hand corner of the photograph), where the last of the New York Indians hung out, like birds on a wire. Where the former inspired grandiose visions, the latter grounded us in the nitty-gritty.

ply yesterday, today and tomorrow. The woman, over whose lap I'm hovering—it's the young Simone Signoret from "A Room at the Top," asleep until that moment—asks with that droll assurance only movie stars have, 'Why so curious?"

"What do you see down there that doesn't go on everywhere?

The plane banks left, tilting our side upward so that in the glare of the late summer sun everything turns white for a second.

"Old times," I say.

"Old times?" she responds, puzzled by the expression.

"The past," I say. "My past."

"Down there? Mais non! Down there is nothing but the present," she says emphatically.

Again the plane banks, to the right this time, and we both look. Simone sees nothing that means anything to her. I spot the unmistakable mass of the tower of my junior high school. When it opened in 1929 (just ahead of the Crash), it caused a stir among the cognoscente. Architecturally and pedagogically, inside and out, the school was seen (by who exactly I don't know) as a 'herald of a new age' in educating us would-be parvenues. Unfortunately the shiny optimism didn't last into our time. We got the physical embodiment of the new age but the philosophy got eaten up by the Depression. On the other hand, it was where I copped my first 'feel' (on a crowded staircase, a moment of tenderness beyond mothercare: I thought love would follow), and then saw 'theater,' maybe for the first time, a high school troupe doing Odets: "Awake and Sing." It was us!

Only we were the class of 1949...

"In France," Simone says, "we separate the past from the present."

"How so? How do you do that?

"We have the Pantheon. Do you know it?"

"The Pantheon? Of course, the palace of the greats."

"Yes, the Pantheon is where we place our heroes."

"Heroes?"

"Yes, those who embody our past."

"I see, " I say, still straining to catch a glimpse of something recognizable in the patchwork of streets down below.

"You don't look convinced."

"It's not that, really. I just wasn't thinking of the past in those terms. What I was thinking of had personal meaning. But a pantheon isn't a bad idea."

The plane banks again and the Bronx streets below, a crazy quilt of intersecting lines, come up at us. I pick up the Boston Post Road where it separates itself from Third Avenue which I could identify by the bridge to the south of it, and follow the road north past where I used to live, all in an instant. In his presidency, Jimmy Carter had visited those streets and had had them declared a disaster area, a symbol of urban decay–there where I used to meet my father coming home from work and where precociously I had shaped an entrepreneurial imagination. 'Had it all simply vanished,' I wondered, squinting to take in the details in the streets below. 'Even the way the boys there grew up?'

From our great height, we kept circling the city.

"A pantheon isn't a bad idea," I heard myself saying again.

Just then the stewardess' voice broke through the white noise of the plane engines as she walked up the aisle asking passengers to buckle up. In a flash, the dream vanished and I came back to myself. The plane came down out of the sky, crossed Flushing bay, and landed. I found my car in the parking lot where I had left it weeks before and drove up to Connecticut. In the evening, after dinner, I took the invitation from its envelope and read it to myself, still thinking about the idea of the pantheon, and about old times, and before I was done my thoughts were tumbling out and racing back in time.

2

Bronx Melodies

I must be a rising three here, and starting to look, sometimes with puzzlement, at the world around me. The pose was generic; a rite of passage. Nearly all of my friends had these faux cowboy pictures on display in their apartments. My mother, like all the other mothers I knew, wanted to inform posterity about her son.

In the pantheon of old times that lives in my mind, at the front of the room where you enter, is the mercurial Bobby Mendelson: clever, curly-haired cherub with a heart of gold, poised in flight, or more often fleeing from the scene of the crime. Ironically, prophetically, I credit Bobby with my introduction to the inner mechanisms of the free enterprise system. In my juvenile period, Bobby defined what it was to be a risk-taker and a maverick. In a place where everybody belonged to teams to secure their social standing–the Marvels, the

Mohawks, the Iroquois, teams whose names were designed to instill awe and passion in the hearts of their opponents–he stood alone, blithe-spirited and unshielded. Somehow he seemed able to create himself out of whole cloth, without group loyalties, while the rest of us only pretended to be independent dealers. Later on, I realized that what made Bobby seem so cavalier about being a maverick distracted him from doing anything about his troubled life, which ended tragically when he was scarcely 30. But back then, he had the charm of the true street urchin. He was also the transgressor *par excellence* of that cardinal tenet of public school life: thou shalt not cut school. Among us New York Indians, cutting school was a true test of courage. Not only was it a transgression, but punishable by God. Bobby, in 5th grade, cut school ostensibly to work on an ice truck. That endeavor alone endeared him to me. He was the embodiment for me of the active principle.

Of course, to truly see Bobby, or to see him truly, you'd need to see the place, preferably in a space that was contiguous: a sea of tenements, five- and six-stories tall–a neighborhood made for the

exploring mind—that ran for as many blocks as the eye could take in. Not the notorious old-law tenements that were produced on the lower East Side in the 19th century. Ours were what the real estate agents referred to as modern housing for workers and their families—or at least housing for workers with modern conveniences.

Some of this housing even had architectural embellishments, with baroque-like lobbies, and—most modern touch of all—elevators with elevator operators. (In one of those classier buildings, in fact, the elevator operator, Andrew, a colored man, as we used to say, would occasionally shoot craps with us for nickels and dimes in the basement between calls for service. And in a sense, it was he, by being the first adult in our lives to treat us so amiably *en masse*, who introduced us to the egalitarian principle. By Andrew hustling us, and letting us hustle him, in those crap shoots, we were brought right in to the heart of American experience without having to be told or read a word about it. It was that kind of place.)

My life in that sea of tenements began on a street just above the Jennings Street market. The Jennings Street market has expired but in that day it was the world to me. In its slight meandering fashion, it was charm itself. Eggs and potatoes. Butter and cheese. Bread and milk. Fruits and vegetables Chickens and fish. Hustle and bustle.

Where the market proper stood, a bunch of narrow streets converged from different points on Boston Road, creating the illusion of a great crossroads, full of meaningful transactions. And on Wilkens Avenue, which intersected the market along its western boundary (where President Carter stood), rows of retail shops operated, including a Woolworth's Five and Ten notorious in its time as an easy mark for juvenile shoplifters.

In all, there may have been 100 businesses concentrated there, in that jumble of streets—immigrant businesses, selling whatever was fresh, moved fast, and sold cheaply. For kids like myself, Jennings Street market was indispensable.

First, the market was the source of some of our earliest American folklore—stories handed down from one generation to another.

Stories about peddlers like Jake the pickle man, who people from miles away came to do business with and who was regarded with both affection and derision simultaneously.

Jake's business occupied no more than an alley the size of one of my wife Dorothy's closets, but what he and his wife did there was pure theater. Backstage was a clutter of barrels of brine, where the pickles were cultured. Front stage was where Jake performed the ritual of selling pickles by the jar. These were conceded to be the best pickles in all Bronx Jewry, and cost only pennies; people were avid for them. Jake supplied the pickles, but you supplied the jar. And

Jennings Street market 1934.

heaven help you if Jake didn't care for your jar. If he didn't like your jar–too small, too big, too thin, too thick–or if he took exception to the way you looked at him, a king's ransom could not induce him to sell you his pickles.

Secondly, my friends and I depended on the market for our supplies: wooden crates, cheese boxes, whatever. They were the materials necessary for our unique accommodation to American street lifestyle. Only someone who in his childhood has transformed a wooden cheesebox into a curbside gambling casino to host a game of chance played in the gutter with marbles will properly understand.

All the boys I played with had these miniature casinos. They operated very simply, at the curb. You cut small holes in the base of the cheesebox–holes slightly larger than a small marble–and dared all comers to score against "the bank." Score and my bank paid out three marbles. Miss the shot and the bank foreclosed (on at least that marble). With a cheesebox, you were magically transformed from a have-not to a have. Plus you learned how to play the "odds," which was not an insignificant lesson in life skills. Finally, it was out of such activities that I made pals. Bobby was one of those pals.

When we were eight or nine, he took me into his confidence: Did I want to make some money? He was buying small packages of Flears double bubble gum for one cent–he had a source of supply even though World War II had limited Flears' production capacity–and he was selling it in the schoolyard for five cents. As far as kids in the schoolyard were concerned, Flears double-bubble gum was the most precious commodity in the neighborhood. Everyone had a craving for it. If a store owner was lucky enough to receive a supply, he could literally sell out in a minute. Bobby came over to my house during lunch one day, filled my hat with the square-shaped delicacies, and we were in business. In those days, school kids went home for lunch, and formed lines in the schoolyard when it was time to reenter the school building. That's when we went into action. The entire operation took no more than a few minutes, even though we charged a 500 percent markup. I learned there the two fundamental aspects of business practice in the free enterprise system:

• If the demand for a product is great, the product's sales price is not material.

• You can't go far wrong if you take in more money than you spend.

I also learned from Bobby how easy it is for the entrepreneurial spirit to sweep its bearers over the edge. The fact is, Bobby had a demon side, and being in his friendship carried with it a certain element of danger, which was an aspect I obviously coveted. One day, he came to me with a pass key for rooms in the school building. How he had come by it, I didn't think to ask, but he proposed sneaking into the school when the Boy Scouts were meeting there on Friday night and ransacking the fifth grade for school supplies: paper, pen-

Principal Goldberger

cils, paper clips, books, and everything else that was left around.

Friday night came and we went ahead with our plan. We pretended we were going to the weekly Boy Scout meeting but went instead to the offices on the second floor. There was no security at the school and we slipped into the principal's office. I can still see the sign over the portal: 'Principal Goldberger.' In my own mind, I registered the warning: Proceed at your own risk! At the most, I told myself, we would look around and leave. We had a plan, although at this point I could not say what it was.

But once in Goldberger's office, our 'plan' fell into disarray. Maybe it had to do with seeing the trappings of authority so accessible, so vulnerable. We morphed into sharks, grabbing things indiscriminately. Before I could think about anything, Bobby had pocketed the principal's fountain pen and taken 20 sets of keys from a desk drawer. By the time we had finished sacking the office, I knew we had done something unforgivable, something for which you could be sent away. If my father found out, it would be death and degradation. As we fled, down the "Up" staircase and out into the night, I felt this love of danger grow into something separate from myself. What we had on us was "hot stuff;" in fact, too hot to hold onto. Weighed down with guilt, we went into the park across the street from the school and buried our swag in a deep hole.

I remember arriving at school that next Monday morning, my heart in my throat. The general hubbub at the school entrance wasn't helping any. Not understanding what it signified, I spent the day in terror. I was sure that Mr. Goldberger would find out what Bobby

and I had done. And where was Bobby? He wasn't even in school to share my misery. Either he had run away, which I briefly considered doing, or he was at work, delivering ice. As it turned out, he was just laying low, which is what any smart operator does after "pulling a job."

It would be weeks before I accepted the fact that we wouldn't be found out. It would be years–just before my *bar mitzvah*–before we had courage enough to dig up the keys and boast of our exploit, and for me the boast would be only half-hearted. It was a while before I gave in again to my instincts for taking risks, and by then I had had a chance to begin considering some alternative models for entrepreneurial activity, most crucially watching my father's business rise and fall.

My father was actually a native-son, born in Manhattan in 1907, but he returned with his parents to Polish Galicia before he was of school age, and didn't come back to New York until after WW I. By then, he was 18 and a genuine greenhorn. But a greenhorn who carried a U.S. passport, spoke six languages, and was ready to take an eye for an eye because of what he had personally experienced of anti-Semitic violence. Short but strong- shouldered, and fearless, he loved telling and retelling the story of how, walking through Chelsea on his way to meet a friend in the fur market one day not long after his re-arrival, he encountered a gang of tough Irish kids who wanted to provoke him: "Sheeny, sheeny! Yeah, yeah! Yer not even white," they taunted him.

The kid who was chief taunter wanted a fist fight, but Morris knew nothing about bare knuckle fighting. To him, that was a gentlemen's game. He grabbed the kid by the throat and would have squeezed the life out of him, had others not intervened. Whether or not this tale was true, it used to seem plausible to me. I saw the intensity he brought to everything that he wanted to manage, whether it was his work, his wife, or his son. There were no half measures. In that regard I am very much his protégé.

He could be violent just as easily as he could be sweet, which some say describes a passionate nature. A couple of times, he nailed me for not towing the line. Not enough for me to lose respect for him, but enough to make an impression on me. He never left me in doubt about his love for me, but at the same time the fights he had with my mother were so intense that I can't remember a time when I didn't fear for their marriage. And knowing his strength—he did physical work all day, moving boxes of bottles and heavy things—I worried that he would get carried away and hurt her. Once, after a serious battle between them, I slept in her bed, armed to the teeth, because he had been drinking and I was afraid the argument would escalate.

My old neighborhood, at Boston Road and Wilkens Avenue, as shown here in a photograph from 1942, was plebian but elegant in understated ways. The open space on the left-hand side of the photograph, circumscribed by a barely discernible chain link fence, is the schoolyard where, in that year, my friend Bobby Mendelson and I ran a black market operation in Flears double bubble gum, which introduced me to the free enterprise system.

Alcohol would set him off. In fact, he drank to excess regularly enough for me to think of him as an alcoholic. Mostly he drank in a neighborhood saloon near the Jennings Street market, like many people do at the end of a workday, putting some space between the day and the night.

By the time I came on the scene, Morris was already established in the delicatessen business, a man trying to go places. He had

Third Ave. before the El was torn down.

moved up in stages from singing waiter to grocery clerk to store manager to small merchant, with his own business on Third Avenue in the East 50s. For a while, as part of it, he ran a cottage industry out of our kitchen, which I participated in. I can still see myself, sitting around the kitchen table, with my father, my mother, and my grandmother, packing cooked onions into small glass containers that Morris took downtown the next day and sold at his shop across from P. J. Clark's.

The comedian, Jackie Mason, does a classic routine about owning your own business. Every Jew wants his own business, even if he's just a small partner. "I'm a partner! I've got a store!" Being in business for my father and for the men of his time and place was like owning a piece of the world. And the place Morris had on Third Avenue was an interesting business because of who his customers were and how he served them. He even drew trade from the Waldorf-Astoria, a few blocks away, which could be counted on every week for orders of dozens of platters of hors d'oeuvres.

After WW II started, diplomats on their way to Europe used to come in and leave money on account, asking my father upon letter request to forward them foodstuffs that were in short supply overseas. When he put a sign in the window, "Overseas Parcels to Europe," the business really took off, and he brought in a partner to help develop it. The partner was some guy shaky from the rackets, but he had money, which the business needed if it was to grow. It became very successful, filling the basement of the store with its activity.

I used to dream about that basement. At the street level, it was a small store, but the basement was enormous. Going from the small space of the store to the large space of the basement was an adventure. In my dreamlife the basement became the Roman catacombs.

But then it turned out that my father's partner was a crook. He began skimming from the overseas accounts and when those customers returned to claim their balances, there was no money to give them.

Things went crazy after that. The store lost its liquor license, business went downhill; and while neither my mother nor I knew anything about it at the time, my father had to borrow money from loan sharks just to stay afloat. It's the classic demise of the man who loses his footing on the economic ladder. We didn't find out about it until two years later, after my father had died, and the loan sharks showed up at our door wanting to be paid.

That period, between the time my father's business failed and his sudden death of a cerebral hemorrhage at age 45, shaped my life. That is when I cut my teeth on the realities of bringing order out of chaos, although I can't say that I mastered the technique right then.

My mother and father, Shirley and Morris, in the late 1930s.

It takes seasoned skills to apprehend the chaos a reckless man can sow.

And if I say my father was a reckless man, I don't mean to be judgmental, or begrudge him his extravagances. I was, after all, often the recipient of that extravagance. But reckless extravagance is what best describes the dominating attribute of his character. He probably was a reckless lover. He must have swept my mother off her feet.

I think they met on a blind date and went dancing. They had different styles of moving on a dance floor, but they both loved to dance, which is one of the first things I noticed about them when I began to see them apart from myself. They were two nimble-footed romantics and I probably take after them.

But where he was loose and reckless, my mother was high-strung and practical. She had grown up in a small town in Russia and was five- years-old when WW I broke out, ten when the Bolsheviks took power, and 11, in 1920, when she emigrated with her mother and sister to the Jewish community in Providence, R.I. Those six years left an indelible mark, although in trying to tell me about her experiences, she mostly kept coming back to the aftermath of the war, when the Bolsheviks took power. The picture she painted was one of almost comic desperation, running from place to place with her family, trying to keep out of harm's way. To a Jew in that time and place, keeping out of trouble could be a difficult matter.

In Providence, she lost her Russian accent, learned English quickly, breezed through the rigorous program at Classical High School, and expected a rich uncle to put her through college. But that expectation never materialized. Another family member got the call, not Shirley; and that became a source of lasting hurt. Instead of going to college, she came to New York and took a job at her Uncle Julius' corset and brassiere salon, "Madame Julius" on West 57th Street. She intended this to be an apprenticeship not just a job; afterwards, she planned to go into business herself, like her sister.

At the time, corsetiering was a promising profession for women. They didn't have the mass market merchandise we have now, so it was like being a custom tailor. Fitting corsets and brassieres was thought of almost as an art form. The store carried only one pre-made brand, which was the top of the line, and they still had to be stitched and fitted. I have a vague memory of the shop. Shirley still worked there for a while after she was married. I remember more of the business she ran at home, after we had moved to Boston Road. Her customers would come to our apartment and go into my parents' bedroom for fittings. I would hear the grunting as they pulled on their corsets. I don't remember lusting after anything I saw there–the women were mostly old, at least to my eyes, but I do recall being curious!

Most of my mother's ideas about gracious living were shaped at Madame Julius. She met society over the counter. And what she saw encouraged her to feel she could fit in very nicely. I guess she saw my father in that light back then. In photographs I have of them, from that time, I can see that they were both very attractive people.

I remember little about my parents entertaining friends at home. Social occasions were usually family affairs, and for most of these we seemed to go someplace, either to Manhattan or to Brooklyn, or the occasional trip to Providence, where my mother's sister, Aunt Marian, and her family lived. Once a year, we were invited to a Passover seder at Uncle Julius', with all the other Juliuses, which was a big deal. He was the patriarch of the family and would give silver dollars to all the kids who came. He liked to talk about the values of education, a theme that, as I got older, my mother promoted, especially on our drives home through Central Park and Harlem. The worth of an education was incalculable, Uncle Julius believed, and my mother agreed.

By the time I was 12, her determination for my success in the world had become tied to my going to college and not being a del-icatessen owner like my father. Fortunately I had already figured this out for myself. Although she said it often in angry tirades directed at my father, she would repeat it even when she was alone with me. It was an idea she wanted to put out there for me to consider, and consider it I did, but not happily. I loved them both; I didn't want anything to happen to either one of them and I didn't want our family to break apart.

Needless to say, my mother's bitter remarks stung my father and, impatiently, he would turn them aside. If he had any insight about the young high-strung woman from Providence he had married, he didn't use it to improve things. Discussions between them were quickly reduced to arguments, and argument piled onto argument. I remember these, often on our late Sunday night drives home, passing through the quiet streets of the city. I was always glad when we reached familiar territory and I could anticipate being in the company of my friends again, hanging out on our corner, talking baseball, being glib, away from my parents and any worldly concerns.

Actually Sundays always began brilliantly for me. I woke to the sound of the Yiddish Hour on the radio, with everyone in good spir-

A broadcast of the Yiddish Hour.

its. My parents were not observant Jews, but they were big on *Yiddishkeit*–Jewishness–and they relished the lyricism and humor of the language, which despite their proficiency in English was second nature to them. It became part of me, as well. I breathed it in. There are times when a half-remembered jingle from the Yiddish Hour will roll off my tongue unbidden. My favorite was a promotion for a clothing store on the lower East Side. It was sung like a routine in a musical comedy:

> *Joe and Paul a fargenigen!*
> *Joe and Paul mir kenst a bargain kriegen!*
> *A suit, a coat, a gabardine!*
> *Bring dein mann, und kleinen ziene!*

Where, at that point in time, could one hear a more felicitous come

Broadway in 1946. A year later, I'd be barmitzvahed on this block.

on? But by nightfall, driving back to the Bronx, Morris would often be drunk, and beyond reason.

I remember his being so deeply in the tank once that he was driving the car on the wrong side of the road. I was more or less convinced we were going to die in a crash. My mother screamed, "You're on the wrong side, Morris!" But he felt, as always, that she was exaggerating the danger, and that he was perfectly capable of driving; so he kept going until finally we arrived home. It was a harrowing experience. And of course at the end of it inevitably there was another argument.

They argued often about money, and they argued about his drinking. Shirley thought that the money Morris spent on cars and on drinking were extravagances we could ill-afford. When it was time for my *bar mitzvah,* they argued for months about how to celebrate it. My mother thought the celebration should be modest. The war had just ended and, while business was good, she felt it could always get bad again. She liked the security of having some savings and she was thinking of the future–money for college–and who knows, maybe I would need help starting my own family. My father thought that was ridiculous. He wanted to celebrate lavishly.

If something new and appealing came along, he wanted to be able to respond to it. He wasn't for squirreling away money, buying things on time. Fatalistically, he would argue in his gruff manner that he might not get to see my wedding. Maybe I'd elope without giving him the *naches* of a wedding. My *bar mitzvah* celebration should be expensive and unique, he felt, and if it took his savings, which it did–and which left Shirley even more unhappy–that's how it would be.

Where my friends' parents hired a hall at one of the local synagogues, or at least a hall somewhere in the Bronx, Morris gave me a *bar mitzvah* party at a hotel on Broadway and W. 46th Street, which was lavish, extravagant, and surely foolhardy. But few who attended ever forgot it, least of all me. I can't think of anything in the city in the first years after the war that was more incandescent than the spectacle of Broadway at Times Square and from there on in, I would always feel part of the place. Broadway not only as geographic destination, but as a measure of what was best.

So many people came to the *bar mitzvah*, with so many gifts, that it was all I could do to stay focused on the speech I had prepared to mark my rite of passage. All the women wore gift corsages. The out-of-town guests were put up at the hotel. And the New York Indians, many of them by then *bar mitzvah* boys themselves, pocketed the loose cigarettes absent-mindedly left at their table and went out onto Broadway to smoke them: their first smokes, and their first night at-large in the city unchaperoned.

In minutes they were blowing smoke rings at the passing throng.

It was the freedom to do things that we found so compelling. But also it was a time to try new things. The streets were crowded with people out on the town, excited, moving, taking in what there was to see and hear, and we were part of it. I thought placing us there was such a generous and dynamic thing for my father to have done that I forgave him his excesses. I knew that you had to be persistent like him if you wanted these things to happen, even as I knew that what was happening would cause bad blood between he and my mother. Such contradiction seemed to be the particular needle I was going to have to learn to thread.

Meanwhile early adolescence had me and the other New York Indians moving around the city, testing our strategic skills against the city's enormity and complexity, but also in a sense taking responsibility for our own education. Having mastered the subway system from where we lived to midtown Manhattan—from the Bronx to Broadway—and other points of interest, we recognized no obstacles. For a five-cent subway ride the world was our oyster. The odd job here and there, and the few cents our parents meted out in weekly allowances gave us all the means we needed.

For one thing, we became adept at crashing the gates at Madison Square Garden to watch hockey matches and college basketball, forcing open the emergency exits at the 69th Regiment Armory where the Knicks played in the first years of the NBA, and scaling the walls at the Polo Grounds, for baseball and professional football games. Enthralled as we were with sports figures, we were not only fans but we got to be close to the action. In turn, that passion led us into autograph collecting. Even more than gate-crashing, collecting the autographs of ball players allowed us to feel part of the game.

Not only did we collect autographs at the Polo Grounds and

Yankee Stadium, both stone's throws from our neighborhood, but having learned at which hotels in midtown each visiting team stayed when they came to town to play the Yankees, the Giants or the Dodgers, we stalked the players there for the signatures we craved.

The game, for us, had more to do with the challenge of "getting" autographs than the business of "collecting" them. Getting autographs from every player on a team was better than getting 100 percent on a school exam. Even though the hotel's house detectives were always trying to sequester us, generally we were quicker to spot them than they us. The experience of outwitting authority was a singular pleasure.

This mania for collecting extended to canceled American postage stamps. I think here it was fed by an impulse to actively embrace the stories of American history that we were growing up with, and not just be instructed about them. North of where we lived, in an area that still breathed that air of the past that the school wanted us to absorb in 'social studies,' we discovered a little storefront shop where we could buy stamps 'on approval,' which was a kind of commercial con that we thought we could turn on its head to our profit, and we would troop there whenever the spirit moved us. Had we minds to look around at where we were, we might have seen there a true embodiment of what we were looking for. Instead we would go to this place, on West Farms Square, at the foot of the train station, trying to get something for nothing, which was a standard for operating without money. What the place itself might have taught us, had we been keen on discovering it, eluded us.

The configuration of office buildings at Rockefeller Center, to which we made after-school and Saturday forays, played a similar educative role for us. We'd go there, from office to office, in search of glossy handouts, the kind that corporate America was beginning to generate to tell their story. Our cover story, in case anyone asked, was that we were doing school reports and needed visual extras. Being able to walk freely through the portals of 30 Rockefeller Plaza, take an elevator to the 30th floor–our Bronx, after all, didn't rise any higher than six stories–and call on the offices of Standard Oil for road maps, annual reports, or whatever else we could name, confirmed for us the exhilarating idea that it was a free country and we could do what we wanted, be what we wanted, and get what we wanted, simply by using our imaginations and going after it. Our escapades had no greater payoff for us than the adrenaline rush of accomplishing something we had thought up to do. The spirit that fueled us as we sped from place to place was not yet defined by making money.

It wasn't until my father's business went into financial hemorrhage and all the help had to be let go, that I got a close look at the downside of the free enterprise system. That was when Morris would open the store in the morning, Shirley would come in to provide relief during the day, and I would come in after school to work until closing time. The store, having lost its license to sell beer, drew very few customers late at night, and it left me with little to do, other than listening to the occasional neighborhood hardluck story from people who wandered in from the cold, more hardup than we were. Being there in such circumstances was draining, humbling, and eye-opening.

Every night for a year, with the meager receipts of the evening in a brown paper bag, I closed the door on a failing business and rode a cab up to the Bronx, asking myself: What could I do to help? How could I make a difference? I really didn't have any answers. No one seemed to have them. We didn't know enough about what could be done to untie the knots. I don't think of myself as ever having been an obsessive kid, but I think at the time I must have become obsessed with that problem. For a long time, a shroud of gloom lay over my soul.

Theodore Roosevelt High School didn't help me much in this regard. It wasn't a progressive academic institution; it never was. The governing idea there was, 'Get these boys and girls out into the world and into jobs that'll permit them to survive.' But I always knew I could survive: it was more than just a job that I wanted. Besides there was never a question in my mind that I wouldn't be going to college. I always felt, whatever else was going on, my parents would find a way for me to go. That was simply my frame of reference. Few of my friends thought otherwise. In the East Bronx, Jews as a group had an almost religious fervor about educating their children. More central was the question of what I was going to do after the formalities of public schooling were accomplished? What would be my calling?

So I worked at being a student, and I wasn't bad at it. I took the courses, the Chemistry, the English, the Math, and I read the books that had to be read. I probably did better in my junior and senior years than I did at the beginning. I had some fairly good teachers. They weren't wasted years. We all thought of it as dues-paying. The real challenges beckoned in the beyond, a subway ride away.

Meanwhile, in spite of the gloom and insecurity, I felt life continue to spin its course, a process in which friends meant everything. There were always activities to be part of, things that we arranged for ourselves, for better or worse. Adults contributed little to any of it. What might have been lost in mature counsel, we gained in becoming resourceful, a quality especially critical in the summer, when not having a job was a small death. In one stretch of summer and fall, maybe the last before I got into accounting, I kept from sinking into the abyss by working as a sales clerk in a brassiere shop in Parkchester, going door to door in Irish and Italian neighborhoods selling commercial paintings of Jesus of Nazareth and, on Saturdays, hustling pennants and badges outside football stadiums as far afield as Philadelphia and West Point.

Crotona Park, where we lived and played into middle adoles-

cence, was fitted out with all kinds of child-oriented public improve-
ments during the early years of the New Deal. For our quarter of the
immigrant Bronx, it stood for Central Park. We played all kinds of
games there, we went fishing in Indian Lake, which was really no
more than a pond, and when the pond iced up in winter we skated
on it, although as I remember it not very gracefully. When my parents were distracted either by the war, or their work, or their anger,
it was to the park that I'd go. The park kept us safe. The playground
that was erected there for us stands in my pantheon in a room all by
itself.

That fall, right after my dad died, I formed the habit of going on
long solitary walks through the park, lost in thought and lonely, trying to figure out my next moves. Trying to get ahead of the hurt I
felt and very conscious of the need to take direction, I'd cross from
our side of the park to where it led into Belmont, an old Italian
neighborhood near my high school, and then I'd walk back, won-
dering all the while about how my mother and I were going to
scramble out of debt, how I was going to put my life together? What
was I to be? What must I do to prepare?

On one level, the transition to college was purely utilitarian. The
City College Business School, on E. 23rd Street in Manhattan, where
I finally decided to go (not that I had many options), had all the
basics of a college, but none of the social amenities or attitudes. No
campus quadrangles, no campus. No Greek societies, no place for
students even to sit and talk, except in the 10th floor lounge or the
11th floor cafeteria. Gramercy Park was nearby but we had no enti-
tlement to its comforts. In fact, the college had just been through a
basketball scandal and the general approach of the place was like a
turtle with its head pulled in. We felt the need to arrive for class as
punctually as possible and to leave afterwards without milling about.
In form and function it was hardly distinguishable from high school,
other than the fact that the building was taller. In academic terms, it
was just another rung up the ladder. A case of the city providing for

its own, but without flourishes.

On the other hand, the transition made a real rent in the seeming seamlessness of my life up until that point, and through that opening a new self emerged. I had had an intuition about it when I arrived at the college that first morning. It wasn't so much a question

Call to first principles, entrance, CCNY Business School, E. 23rd St.

of reinventing myself; it was more like apprehending a second identity waiting in the wings, and in the weeks that followed my intuition was borne out. It had something to do with the realization of being free of baggage from the past, almost like an immigrant. What I did or didn't do in a ballgame against the Harlem River A's in the summer of 1945, when I was 10, or in some obscure basketball game in Crotona Park, was no longer germane. I could put all of that behind me and concentrate on what lay ahead. I was *tabula rasa*. It was the beginning of adulthood.

I maintained my boyhood friendships, but I started to develop a new circle of friends. They weren't that different from the boys I had known all my life; in fact, demographically they were probably the same. But there was something about being there with them, in that early phase of professional vetting that was inspiring. I could see them differently just by virtue of being seen differently myself. It was as if someone with a big brush was coating us over with special varnish, consecrating us for a mysterious task that had yet to be decided. In a couple of years, we would never be seen again as we were–except when we came together.

We came by subway–early morning rides from the far reaches of the city; mostly Jewish boys like me, many from the Bronx, many from my own neighborhood, the salt of the earth, carrying our lunches in brown paper bags saved from yesterday's groceries. Those of us who had cars were never sure their engines would last another month.

But while we didn't have much in the way of annuities, and were pretty provincial, we were a protean lot, ready to make good, and full of enthusiasm. If we accepted our slightly surreal situation with good nature, underneath beat intensity of purpose. The sons of fur workers, coatmakers, tie makers, storekeepers, garment workers, house painters, we were heading for the corporate world, although I doubt many of us were thinking in those terms: I wasn't. Intellectually I was just making the shift from having comic book heroes to reading *The New York Times.*.

Riding downtown on the El, there were always four or five of us, and always in the end car to catch the swerve, and the feeling of danger, as we whipped around Dead Man's Curve at 125th Street, high over Harlem, to head down the east side. I especially remember that turn in the winters, with the train wheels screeching, and the sensation of one's life hanging by a thread. Once there was a fire in the train at that juncture and the train had to be boarded by firemen on ladders raised from the street. "Don't be nervous," the firemen said as they clambered into our car, suspended high above no man's land. "Be calm."

But who was nervous about a fire? We had just whipped around Dead Man's Curve. And besides, we were trying–standing there–to finish school assignments due that morning. "What's the solution to the problem on page 27?" "Can you make sense of what this guy is asking us to do on page 32?"

Instead of fraternities, we belonged to House Plans–social clubs whose principle function was to organize weekend parties. From a cultural perspective, our house was probably one of the more backward assemblies; it was called Sachs '56. The parties never amounted to much. I can't remember any classic romances emerging. When it came to the gentlemanly arts, we had the simple reputation of being boorish. The romantic passions of our members were expressed at that time in base terms. No matter what happened, it was always with a sense of relief that I said goodnight to my dates, and with a sense of glee that I regrouped later in the evening with my crowd so that we could tell each other how we had done.

Most of my dates centered around going to the movies. The movie business was in its classic period: John Wayne, Henry Fonda, Gregory Peck, Barbara Stanwyck, Bette Davis, John Garfield, Paul Muni, Jimmy Cagney were all in their formative years. In very simple ways, those and the other stars of that era reflected all the hopes and dreams we had. The Loew's Paradise on the Grand Concourse was as much of a movie palace to us as the Paramount Theater in Manhattan. Taking a date to the Paradise and then for an ice cream frappe at Krum's across the Concourse was like being 'in the action' and about as much as our limited funds could afford.

Such modest social pretensions made for a bare bones college life, but on the plus side was the fact that later, when we got to work in the field of our professional concentration, there wasn't much baggage to distract us, or to slow us down. There were 30 or 50 kids in a class. We were expected to do the work. If we failed the final, we failed the course. If someone failed often enough, they were dropped from the school. There were always others waiting to take your seat. There were no student advisors for counseling about academics or troubles at home. If you lost your footing–even if only through clumsiness–you were out.

In my second year, all of twenty-years-old, I made the fateful decision to major in accounting. I wasn't sure I wanted to end up in public accounting, but I thought accounting would be a great background for whatever it was that I'd want to do. An uncle of my mother's was the senior partner in a big firm of public accountants, and in the back of my mind I thought I'd be able to get a job with him. Not only had he started this firm from nothing and built it into something substantial, according to family lore, he was a celebrity in his own right for testifying in a famous fraud case. To me, he seemed almost a romantic figure.

But more practically, I'd been exposed to a sampling of business courses–marketing, statistics, sales management–and all of them seemed to me like meaningless kinds of study. Accounting, on the other hand, seemed to be a useful tool. It was the lingua franca of business. Armed with it, I could move in many directions.

The faculty were all prominent in the profession. Their pedagogy was intertwined with real business practices developing right outside the doors of the school. New York City's postwar economy, circa early 1950s, was beginning to build up. It seemed to add up. I started to visualize a way out of the family financial crises following my father's death. I'd found my path.

In my junior year, I had a program that fitted my needs. I spent all day in classes on Mondays and Tuesdays, and until noon on Wednesdays. For the rest of the week, which included Wednesday afternoon, and all of Thursday, Friday and Saturday, I worked for Kahn & Shore, a small accounting firm of the two principals. They were my first teachers and I was their junior. It was perhaps one of the worst practices in the city, but working with them was an experience that prepared me for everything that followed in my business career, and then some. It wasn't so much a foundation that was laid; bedrock is the better term. All for which I was paid the handsome sum of $1 an hour. Very quickly I was working more hours than I was going to school. Not only had I found my path, I was launched.

The clients were mostly contractors in the garment industry, many of them immigrants, really marginal operators who were making maybe $100 a month more than their business employees. And

South Bronx

the sweatshops that they operated out of were grim manufacturing lofts in the South Bronx in buildings with very few amenities.

The South Bronx hadn't yet become notorious as a symbol of urban blight; the term Fort Apache as a name for the place hadn't yet been coined. It was, however, pretty much down at the heels. It had always been a tough area, even when the buildings were new. I could see how it would have intimidated a stranger. But I had grown up on the streets nearby and I felt a sense of connection to the place.

Two years earlier, as an 18-year-old, I might not have been allowed to pass through without having to defend myself. Now my briefcase stuffed with papers identified me as a benign figure. In fact, I could be seen as someone who did some good in the neighborhood. I was the guy who made out the payroll. If I didn't get through to make the payroll, mothers and fathers wouldn't get paid. With two sweatshops a day to cover, I may have been the fastest payroll clerk in America.

Wedding, 1956. The groom, to my right, was the first of the NY Indians to marry.

I still had my baby face, but Kahn said: "When you go into these places, you are the man. You are the accountant. If you say St. Louis is in California, then St. Louis is in California, period." And Shore, sizing me up, said: "You'll be on your own most of the time; what do you think is the most important thing to do when you go to a client?"

"Reconcile the bank balance?

"Nooo..."

"Treat the client with respect?"

"Nooo..."

"Dress well?"

Well, what was the most important thing? I finally asked. In chorus, they said: "Get our check!" They had a barrel of clients who paid them monthly retainers of $25, $40, $50 a month. "On the first of the month, write our check! Everything else comes after. Whether the hoodlums in the street let you live or not; whether the clients want you back or not, get the check!" Those were the ground rules.

Of course, part of the ground rules was that my bosses could exploit my time shamelessly. During tax season, I'd put in all kinds of hours for which they would keep promising a bonus: "We'll do it like the big firms; we'll work the tax season as if time doesn't mean anything and then we'll reciprocate with a bonus." Needless to say, I never saw that bonus.

Still I was happy enough getting the week's pay; and for all the craziness I had to put up with from my two mentors, or maybe because of it, those were formative years. I was really conscientious, I was learning, I was good at the work that had to be done. Being out there and handling everything, telling people that St. Louis was in California, reconciling their bank balance, and once every while suggesting an idea that would make the operation run more smoothly, gave me a sense of presence. Trying to make order out of what was virtual chaos would serve me well later when I started to handle the business affairs of entertainers who lived in chaos.

The garment workers worked on piece goods. There might be a dozen operations on a garment and each one had a different price. When an operator finished a "lot," she was given a ticket and I had to figure out the value of the tickets. And, of course, very few of the work crew—mostly country women from Puerto Rico—trusted the system to come up with the right tally. They wouldn't accept a mistake, especially one not in their favor.

There was no office. I would work on a wooden box and a makeshift desk that the owner, as an afterthought, bought for $5. Usually space was made for me near the steam press, which was constantly exhaling humid fog while I was there. Bent over my papers

Chelsea loft

and chits, I'd disappear and reappear in the mist.

They were helter-skelter businesses, contractors for larger operations, management one step above labor. And all of them, it seemed, were on the verge of bankruptcy in their own right. In those days, an entire sewing plant cost between $1,000 to $2,000. The only investment needed to begin operations was enough capital for the first week's payroll because it was a payroll business. The manufacturer paid the contractor weekly for whatever was produced. The hardest thing for a guy like me to do in those circumstances—and the most incredible as far as the clients were concerned—was to work up a bank balance. When the contractors wrote checks, many times they never bothered to record them. Talk about working with unknowns: there were no account books! As Kahn and Shore would remind me when I showed my astonishment, "In accounting school or law school, you're given a set of facts and asked to find the answers. In the world outside of school, everybody knows the answer; finding the facts is the problem!"

Cutting my teeth on the idiosyncratic business practices of Kahn & Shore's humble group of clients, I got so I could virtually reconstruct any kind of financial records, and do it pretty accurately. Modesty and earnestness kept me from getting a swell head about it. At the same time, my precociousness didn't go unnoticed. And for that, I was grateful. People forget that even accountants need encouragement, especially young novices.

I remember well the praise of a butcher in the middle of the Bronx, a client of Kahn & Shore's, whose eye I caught. I checked in with him half of one day a week to keep his records current. His shop was big and fully-used; every surface had a greasy patina. The account books would slide off my desk, and I would slide off my chair. The owner, a big, gruff man, never said much to me. But one day, he came in while I was there literally balancing his books, and he said, "You're a good accountant!"

"How can you tell?" I asked. "You don't know."

"I can tell," he said. "When I hire a butcher, I can see the way he uses the meat cleaver. I like the way you hold a pencil. You go for authority. You write numbers like I cut meat." Like Oprah Winfrey, I no longer eat much meat, but the butcher's metaphor has stayed with me.

In the 1950s, accounting had little of the professional cachet that the legal profession had. In fact, it had none at all. In New York, the Jewish accountant was a stock figure of ridicule. It was only later on, when the world of finance went into high orbit and began to reach into accounting departments for its chief executive officers that the image changed, and even then, in the popular imagination, accountants didn't rate too highly. Forty years ago, it certainly wasn't the way into the executive suite. The route forward in the corporate world then was through sales and marketing. The presidents of huge corporations were always the super salesmen. That was the most important part of any business, and it is still the case. Without sales, you have no business; everything else supports that activity. Sales, and maybe engineering, as well as planning: success always starts with an idea.

When the tax laws of the 1960s and 1970s became more sophisticated and finance became more intricate, the big corporations sought more and more of their corporate officers from the controller's office, with more emphasis placed on mergers and acquisitions, and subsequently on leveraged buy-outs. There was a premium placed on talented and reliable corporate financial people, and the accounting profession grew, both in financial and professional status.

But in the mid-1950s when I left CCNY, accounting had the least clout of all the professions. I knew that, and I thought about it; all of us in Sachs '56 did. But we accepted the situation with humor and optimism. We had no social pretensions. We'd beat the odds.

At home I still kept pace with the friends of my childhood, some of whom were going places. No invidious distinctions were made. Home was a landscape of fixed values for us. I certainly didn't question its balance; I didn't want to change it. Whatever desire I had to change things and make myself more self-reliant I projected onto my circle downtown. Downtown we laughed at the strides City College was making in redirecting our entrepreneurial inclinations from potentially criminal to productive career patterns. Living the transformation from month to month absolutely regaled us.

I think we laughed about it, as much as we did, as a way of reducing the anxieties of making the next step, which always seemed problematic. Laughter was as much our sustenance as water is for fish. But that's probably true for adolescents in general, if they're given half a chance to understand themselves.

On the other hand, what I did on the job with Kahn & Shore was very real to me. As Kahn and Shore would say, in instructing me, "on the job meant being in charge," which was an idea I had no problem with. Even though I looked more like 12 than 20, on the job I exuded authority. Not despotic authority; it was more like that of the family doctor who made house calls. I tried to give Kahn & Shore's clients the same kind of assurance.

If the clients had major problems, they might try to reach Kahn or Shore, but basically I was their accountant. They relied on me to solve their business problems, which I really understood. The classic stories may have been about the impoverished worker being put

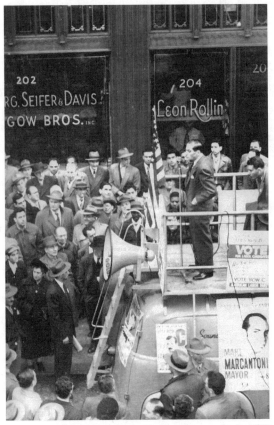

Vito Marcantonio, my mother's hero, campaigning '52.

upon by the selfish boss, but I knew that the reality was slightly more complicated, and that here the bosses were struggling too, working just as hard as, if not harder than, the people they employed.

The garment business is an especially difficult industry. Yet in the 1950s, it was possible, with some luck, to open up a plant with very little capital and go from being broke to doing well, which is how I defined the American Dream. It was a fantasy that I wanted to apprehend for myself, as well. So whenever I came around, I was made to feel important because whatever I did or said was taken seriously, and regarded as important. Not that my advice was always applied. But it was enough for me that, in the midst of the chaotic operating conditions of many of these businesses, people stood still long enough to hear what I had to say.

And the crazier, more *meshuggenah* the settings, the more endearing the people were to me. When I would say to myself, 'There but for the grace of God go I,' it was no empty sentiment. In fact, I would say, 'There go I!' Because if the truth were known, I was crazy, too. I belonged to a House Plan full of crazies. Perhaps a tribeful.

One of the garment industry crazies, Alex Vetcher, a Russian immigrant, earns a place in my pantheon as the bridge I crossed over into my own business. Alex ran a frame-covering operation that subcontracted work from handbag manufacturers. In those days, handbags were put together on metal frames that snapped open and closed. Whether the bag was made with cloth or skin, before the body could be attached, the frame had to be covered with material and fastened with a plastic machine glue, which is what Alex's business did. It was a basic process involving simple machinery, but of course even simple machinery can be complicated to the people who run it. In fact, most of Alex's work crew were Puerto Rican women, about my age, who knew only enough about machinery to operate their particular station.

What made Alex crazy, besides the fact that his business situation wasn't sound, was his love of these ladies, and when he wasn't carrying on about business, yelling and screaming, he tried to make love to every one of them. When I first came to his place, he was carrying on a torrid affair with Gloria Ruiz, a Latin beauty of maybe 19 years, who I lusted after myself. He, too, liked to laugh about his situation; we laughed together. I was in the struggle with him–the struggle to stay alive–and he knew that, and loved me for it. I felt that way pretty much with all my clients.

Meanwhile the seasons passed. My junior year blended into my senior year. College life came to an end. And with it a strategic sense of the possibilities surfaced. Just after graduation I decided to switch firms. I'm not sure I knew where I was going, but I knew that in order to qualify for the CPA exam, I would need to apprentice for another three years–a kind of purgatory–and the idea of doing it at Kahn & Shore struck me as slightly absurd. I realized that if I stayed with them, I'd be ruined forever; I'd become a "schlock accountant," and never learn more than how to handle the minor accounting problems that came up, and how to handle people who were struggling. Those were valuable experiences in themselves, but not the same as creating something of my own, which is where my ambitions were leading.

At that point, I tried to use the family connection to get a job, but one of the junior partners in my cousin's accounting firm saw my interests intruding on his and cut me off at the pass. However, to show me how nice a guy he really was, he steered me to a firm of similar stature and structure. Eisner & Lubin promptly took me in. The big, mainline firms in those days, like Price Waterhouse and Peet Marwick & Mitchell, had quotas for hiring Jews, and it went without saying that Jewish accounting students from CCNY need not apply. If you were any good, the best you could hope for, in the way of employment, was a job with a medium-sized firm, no more than 200 employees, of which New York had a fair number. Eisner & Lubin was typical.

In terms of business organization, my new job was a step backward. What needed to be learned at that point in the practicum–namely auditing technique–I had already integrated into what I was doing for Kahn & Shore's clients. As an Eisner & Lubin junior, I went out with a team to audit company records: specifically to see that their accounting departments were functioning properly, and that the client's books of account were correct. For me, it meant doing bank reconciliations and vouching bills; determining that the facts, which were all there, were put in the right order, and dealing with problems that I knew from the ground up. You didn't have to be a genius to do it, but if you hadn't done it before, as was the case with the majority of my junior colleagues in the firm, the problems could appear monumental.

In these bureaucratic settings, it was hard to come up with answers when things didn't add up. As a junior in this caste-like system, access to the financial statements of these firms was limited, bordering on nonexistent. The corporate personnel treated juniors as they would an interloper. I came into their offices and made requests–I needed a desk, a place to work–and they regarded me as a thorn: an inspector who is auditing their work and asking them to get 'stuff.' It wasn't that they treated me badly; rather they suffered my presence poorly.

When I complained to the senior staff about the long hours and low pay that apprenticeship required, they would stop me in my tracks. They were still working on the feudal principle: dawn to dusk for base pay, which in my case was $65 a week. "*I* never made *any* money!" they would say, "and now you're making $65 a week? What are you complaining about? It's a living wage!"

If I hadn't seen the humor in the setup, I would've cried.

But more important than having a sense of humor, and much more significant, was the fact that on the sly, beneath the light of the silvery moon, I had begun my own accounting practice. Some grand design in my head was unfolding, born out of the same set of gambler's instincts that had marked my adolescent escapades, but schooled now. First of all, Kahn and Shore owed me for the bonuses promised. Had I received the money, as promised, I might have operated differently. But being out of pocket, my choices were limited. We live in a relational world. So, when I left their employ, I took with me the willing Alex Vetcher, owner of Al's Frame Covering Company, as my first client.

If my budding sense of professional demeanor made me feel uneasy about what I was doing, my impulse to right a wrong overcame any rationale. Besides I knew Kahn and Shore would never care about what I had done. Alex was just one of 100 clients from whom they received small monthly retainers; his $25 would not be missed. For me, the acquisition of Alex's patronage was a milestone.

With Alex's company in my portfolio, I went to Steve Burn who had been my classmate at CCNY for four years, and whose business sense I valued above all others, and proposed a partnership. Steve was also a Bronx boy and cut from the same cloth, although from the more organized housing precinct of Parkchester, just north of where I lived. Our personalities and temperaments were studies in contrast, but that probably explains why, in the 25 years that we worked together, we were such a good match. On graduation, he had also taken a job with a middle-class accounting firm, and wasn't long in figuring out the limits.

We met somewhere in the garment district, examined the possibilities of what we might do together, and shook hands on it. The audaciousness of our plans convulsed us in gales of laughter as we wandered home through the streets that night. Our laughter was silent against the din of the hustle and bustle, but the pleasure we felt was not less for its obscurity.

3

Starting Out

Part of going into my own business had something to do with the idea of following in my father's footsteps and making whole what had broken for him, as if that's ever possible. Part was simply putting the neighborhood ideal of being your own boss into practice. On our corner, in our youth, all of the New York Indians aspired to that autonomy. That autonomy, for us, was the American Dream incarnate. The local entrepreneurs–grocers, butchers, bakers, candy store operators–were our civic heroes. We never lacked for models.

At City College, we were taught right away that you could go into business for yourself by buying a practice, or part of one, the way doctors and dentists do, or by working up a practice from scratch, client by client; and that each client was a saleable asset, something, in other words, that could be capitalized. If a client paid you $50 a month, that was $600 a year–the capitalized value, which you could sell, like buildings are sold, say at three to 10 times earnings. The bigger the client base, the greater the golden goose at retirement. Of course, all of that was theoretical. It wasn't a simple matter to sell a practice. But that formulation was something to shoot for. It seemed to say that how you started out didn't matter so much. More important was how you ended up. It was a case of the whole being greater than the sum of its parts.

In its formative years, Burn & Thau, CPAs, would do anything we had to do to serve a client. One client, a woman who owned two or three restaurants, made us sit in the cashier's window whenever we came to do the books, and take cash from her customers, while she fiddled with food preparations in the kitchen or some similar distraction. And we'd do it, mostly dreading that we'd be recognized by some other client passing by.

On the other hand, the concept we were projecting–our professional image, so to speak–was that we weren't only accountants; we were part of the team. We were offering expertise across-the-board: financial and otherwise. With us, a client had not only an accountant, but a company controller. We didn't just show up to report profit and loss! We were there to help the business be successful; whatever it took. We might seem like "Sammy Glick" knockoffs, taking cash, shipping goods, etc., but we also devised financial schemes to keep our clients on track with their dreams.

And, of course, when these dreams were fierce and inspired, as in Alex Vetcher's case, they stretched us to the edge of conventional accounting practice and wisdom! For one thing, Alex could never afford to send the IRS the payroll taxes that he deducted from his employees. He was so close to the edge that his business needed to operate on that money. To do what the government wanted would mean going under. So he simply decided to withhold the money, and wait for the IRS to send a tax examiner around, which might take them as long as two years. Today, Alex would go to jail, but in those days the IRS was more lenient. When an examiner finally came around to say that Alex owed the government for two years of payroll taxes, it was simply left to us to work out payment arrangements that he could manage. The idea, of course, was that time was all that was needed to stabilize Alex's business. We were simply playing for time.

But stay, as Shakespeare would say. There was another story folded into that story. In his frustrations over the IRS's demands for payroll taxes, one day Alex had simply disposed of his books of account, such as they were. He had received notice in the mail of the IRS's intention of sending an auditor, and within a week the books of account had vanished. Alex claimed to have lost them; I think he burned them. So using our work sheets, Steve and I had to reconstruct the books from scratch, and do it fast. Not only because the auditor was coming, but because we were getting only $25 a month from Alex, whether we worked five hours or 100.

We made one journal entry for an entire year's cash receipts, debiting cash and crediting the various income accounts; we made one entry for disbursements, which covers every business expense; we did the same for a second year's worth of operations; and then we held our breath. The IRS agent was a suit-and-tie man, and I could tell immediately he was accustomed to being involved in more big-time audits.

I could tell, too, that he wasn't happy about the working conditions at Alex's place. The loft was dirty, and Alex's crew was running around, yelling across the shop floor in Spanish, often coming by to exchange greetings with me. It was lunchtime, too, and people were breaking out supplies and actually cooking meals. It wasn't merely lunchtime in the garment district; it was lunchtime as enjoyed in Mayaguez, or Ponce, where people sing songs and laugh and cook at mealtime.

I tried to make it as comfortable for the auditor as I could; after all, he could only hurt us. While I watched and tried to appear nonchalant, he read through the journal entries for 1959-60 and then looked up at me. In accounting terms, he didn't believe what he was looking at; but there it was. Besides he could see that there was going to be nothing to collect for the IRS; that was the important consideration. So after ten minutes he closed the books, laid them gently down on the desk, and with his hat and coat walked out, which was the only reasonable thing to do. The incomprehensible had been made comprehensible and he was bright enough to see that if he tried to dig out what had happened, it would only result in a horror story. Alex's crisis had passed. It was an act of grace. Our fame spread.

Not surprisingly, the first six clients we had were all small firms involved in some aspect of manufacturing handbag frames. Alex Vetcher would recommend us to them and they in turn would recommend us to others, all companies as underfunded and desperate to stay afloat as Alex's. I became so familiar with the business that when I saw a woman walking down the street with a handbag, I could tell at a glance how much the bag cost and where the material came from. Six clients, then seven. Then nine, then 10. I felt like King of Handbags.

In fact, even though we were still basically a moonlighting operation, still existing hand to mouth, our assemblage of clients in handbags led us into our first experiment in entrepreneurial diversification. In practical terms, it was like veering off the main highway to take in the local byways; we thought we could make a killing.

Since our clients were always underfinanced, they neither had money nor a bankable relationship. So when there was difficulty over cash flow, some companies would sell off their receivables–the documents of obligation that passed between buyers and sellers–to financial agencies known as factors. Perhaps the companies our clients had shipped to were slow in paying, and our clients, with marginal operations, had to get their hands on cash quickly, which the factors provided. The factors paid something less than 100 percent of what the receivables were worth, depending on how much trust they placed in the manufacturer, or on how much confidence there was in the client and his business. Some paid 80 percent of receivables assigned, others 70 percent, at very high rates of interest. In another time, these high rates would have been deemed unlawful.

The banks charged seven or eight percent for loans, if approved. But if you couldn't borrow money from a bank or get a loan from a relative, and if you wanted to stay in business, you resorted to a commercial factor. It was fairly standard practice in the garment industry.

The factors took chances, too. Even though they had legal possession of the accounts receivables, they gambled on being paid. Frauds were not uncommon. When an owner was desperate enough, it wouldn't take much to inspire him to write up bogus receivables and send them to a factor. In the fast-paced business operations of the city, men were made desperate every day, and swindles were hard to rectify.

By the time Steve and I had nine or 10 of these clients, we had become pretty knowledgeable about factoring and figured we would make more money doing our clients' factoring than doing their books of account, such were the ironies of the business we were in. It was just too tempting an opportunity to let go by. Opportunity,

Garment center, 1958.

we'd heard, only knocked once. So we scraped together $1,000 and formed Dynamic Factors.

At the time, we were still without an office, calling on clients in their dimly-lit lofts in Chelsea after our day jobs had ended.

Accountants could do that—we could sit in the window of a *bodega* during the tax season doing tax returns—without compromising the appearance of professional authority. As factors though, we needed an address; it wouldn't do to be seen as floaters or thought of as fly-by-nights. Steve still had a Bronx address, which didn't have the right rub for a factoring operation, but my mother, my grandmother, and I had just moved to Inwood in upper Manhattan, where the address was 5009 Broadway. Few people knew that 5009 Broadway was closer to Yonkers than to Times Square; to most Broadway was Broadway. So we gave Dynamic Factors a Broadway address to complete the picture and opened a bank account for it with working capital of $1,000. It wasn't much to begin with, but only our incredulous bank officer knew the story.

The key to the whole operation was withholding Dynamic Factors' phone number. This was long before telephone answering machines had become standard household items, and my grandmother, who was always at home, couldn't be counted on to carry out our subterfuge. Our operation depended on very formal exchanges of information that we initiated and controlled at all times. We had to carry out roles like actors in a play.

Of course, every once in a while something would go awry. A client would somehow get hold of my phone number in Inwood and get my grandmother on the phone:

"Dynamic Factors? I want to check a bill."

"Dymic Fecter?" my grandmother would say, repeating what she'd heard. Then all understanding would be lost in the bilingual exchange that followed, and when the caller would reach me later— "I called your number and got a crazy woman on the phone"—I would have to dissemble: "You must have had the wrong number."

In any case, Dynamic Factors was short-lived. After a bit, we saw the folly in what we were trying to do, and parachuted out. Actually part of it was that the handbag business was changing, and some of our clients simply closed down. Frame bags went out of style. Women started to buy clutch bags, and clutch bags didn't use much of a frame. The same new technology that permitted the styles to evolve also made it possible to streamline plant operations. It had become possible for the handbag makers to have the frame-covering stage of production done in-house and middlemen like Alex Vetcher were being phased out.

For awhile the floating game we were playing, operating out of phone booths and office lobbies, threatened to consume me: the IRT, the BMT, Alex Vetcher, the handbag business, Dynamic Factors, the Defense Department, Eisner & Lubin, the late night newspaper headlines, the early morning breakfast joints, uptown and downtown, and loyal partisans–Steve and I–in the middle of it, racing after the electric rabbit like a pair of greyhounds running around the track. Then one day, adding up our assets, we found we had accrued enough of a practice of small clients to rent our first office. We took a very small suite of rooms in the Lincoln Building on 42nd Street in the heart of Manhattan. It was like a having a baby. Proud fathers, we gave each other cigars to celebrate.

In the beginning, not surprisingly, it was touch and go. We probably should have waited another year. Our objective circumstances couldn't always sustain payment of the rent on time. But a lawyer who had taken a shine to us, as we had to him, convinced us that if we were working out of the same office building, he'd send business our way worth triple the rent we'd be paying; it sounded good. He must have thought we would be paying an incredibly low rent because after we moved to his building in the financial district we heard very little from his quarter.

However, there we were. Sometimes we didn't have enough money to make the rent until the 15th of the month. We'd avoid the rent collector from the first to the 15th by coming into the office only at night. Having a secretary–someone to answer the phone and do some typing–improved the situation because the landlord's agent wouldn't hassle her and we could communicate by phone. But the sense of being under siege kept us in its grip for years. It went on for so long, I sometimes forgot it was there. I remember the day I went down into the street after our situation had improved and suddenly became curious about the building, as if seeing it in its wholeness for the first time. It was a Sunday and we had just come into some money. I wanted to take in the surroundings so as to enjoy the moment more and discovered that our building itself was a work of stunning architecture. Until then, we had been like hunted creatures, never stopping to look at the flowers.

It was our clients who really sustained us. One in particular supported us for years: Salvatore Figundio, a machinist by trade. He ran the F & W Machine Shop in the Red Hook section of Brooklyn, which made handbag frames and performed minor engineering operations. His shop was my Pittsburgh, a foundry and a factory in one. When I first met him, he was just splitting up with his partner Mitchell. Sal and Mitchell had had it with each other, but they each wanted to keep our services, which was great. More of that, I thought, and we'd soon be home free. Steve handled Mitchell and I handled Sal. We even battled over their separation agreement, wanting to get the best deal for our respective clients.

Sal was deeply in debt. He owed easily $100,000, which was due immediately. And he had no assets. I had barely reviewed the situation, when he wanted to know my strategy.

"Well, what are we going to do?" he wanted to know.

"I've got two words for you," I said. "Chapter Eleven." He wasn't amused.

"I'm Italian," he said, "we don't do Chapter Eleven! We don't go in for that! I'm going to pay off all these bills!"

"You owe out $100,000, they'll never let you pay it off," I argued. "You have to have credit to..." Before I could finish, he cut me off.

"No, we're going to work on this, you and I, and I'm going to make some money. I'm going to pay off these old debts and meanwhile we'll pay the new bills."

Theoretically that was the way to do it, and Sal really believed he could manage it. But it doesn't always work out that way. Creditors are not always willing to cooperate. They sue, they get a judgment, they get a credit guy in pursuit, and each of these actions can snuff out a business at any time. Sal , though, was adamant.

"No. You're going to come to me once a week, and help me do this. We'll figure out who to pay and we'll work it out."

All week long, Sal would stall his creditors and refuse their calls, giving them only the message that his controller would be in at the end of the week. And when I'd come on Friday, I'd be deluged with calls threatening and pleading. I had worked out payment plans for everyone, but we could rarely meet them.

"Look, we're going to give you $50 this week."

"I'll take $50 a week."

We'd miss a week.

"Hey, *gumba,* what happened?"

"We can't pay $50. We'll give you $30."

"Oh yeah? Well, we're suing."

I'd end up with lawyers and city marshals on the other end of the phone, trying to figure out how to respond to a judgment.

It was a stressful situation, but Sal paid us $75 a week, which made him seem like the golden goose. On the other hand, it wasn't always clear when the money would actually change hands. I'd get a check for $75, but I couldn't always deposit it. In fact, I always had Sal's checks stacked up five, six deep, like phantom planes waiting to land on an unmarked runway. Sal had an amazing relationship with his bank. The banker was probably a local guy like Sal, and would call him and say, "Sal, we've got checks totaling $1,000; you've got $500 in the bank. Who do you want to pay?" "Bounce those checks," he'd say, "and run these others through!" And eventually he would let one of my stacked checks land. He knew that Steve and I needed the money.

In fact, he always took me to lunch on the day I came, as if to make sure I was well-fed for at least one meal during the week.

Between noon and 1, we'd close up the office and go out to an Italian restaurant in the neighborhood, where I would eat two days worth of food. And later in the afternoon, in the growing twilight after all our work was done, he would bring out his guitar and teach me chord structures. Even though his hands were always black with

Lanza's restaurant.

machinery grease, in his heart he yearned to be a classical guitarist, and I wished it for him, too.

There was something else about him that I admired. Despite his being only one step ahead of the sheriff, who was coming on fast, Sal always kept a new Cadillac parked out front, bought on time, which of course made him look more prosperous than he actually was. I was still in an early phase of my social development and the good-looking women who crowded around Sal's place for rides in his car left an impression on me.

"How come Sal," I asked one day, "I'm better-looking than you are, I've got a college degree, and I'm a professional man, but you've got all the women?" He looked at me for a long time, as if I were a young calf–which in many respects I was–and said knowingly, "The woman hasn't been born yet who has seen an ugly millionaire.

4

The High Priestess of Soul,
the Crown Prince of Droll

Gershwin said he was inspired by the sound of the immigrants in the city's streets; I can identify with that. We'd be out on the playground in Crotona Park playing softball or basketball and someone would pass by carrying a portable radio–this was before the age of ghetto blasters–with the tightly structured sound of a Latin percussionist streaming out of it. It was like hearing some exotic bird in the wilderness just after the sun has risen. I suppose in some strange manner this was our wilderness and that was our birdsong. It would hang there, on the wing, for a moment, and then it would float by. Only for a moment maybe, but enough to register. And involuntarily, out there on the diamond, patrolling our positions, we would move to the beat; bah-bah-bah, bah-bah-bi-bah. A little meringue, a little cha-cha. We might have been provincial naifs; closed-in and lacking in regard to high culture. But musically, we were riding a range crisscrossed with streams of complex musical traditions, which came in on the ear whatever else our elders were bent on teaching us. I always regarded as part of my heritage Charlie Parker and Machito, as much as Moisha Oysher. I would have needed to be deaf not to be affected by the sounds surrounding us.

What I remember about it, more formally, is that when I was 12 and my mother and father had a little extra money, my mother decided that there was something lacking in my education and started me on the piano, which was patently ridiculous. I always felt that in order to play the piano well, I would have had to start playing at around the age of eight or younger. But she was determined that I learn to express myself musically. She even took the time to teach me how to dance properly, and she was a good teacher. My dancing was for a long time one of the few social graces I could claim. When she went downtown to see "Oklahoma" on Broadway, she took me with her to make sure I had a chance to see something I could aspire to. She continually made efforts to broaden my cultural horizons.

As part of this uplift program, Shirley bought me an old upright for about $50 and I started lessons with a young woman who was probably a professional performer herself and giving lessons to kids in the Bronx to pay her rent while she struggled for the chance to make good. Unfortunately I was never very good myself; I can say that uncategorically. My fingers gripped the keyboard like a baseball. But I played with incredible gusto, she told me. On at least one occasion, I was offered as an example of 'energetic' musicianship to a younger student. I attacked the keyboard. I banged on it. In my hands, basic Bach and Beethoven fused with 20th century impatience. That energy—which is who I was—issued from me no matter what was called for by the musical arrangements.

Of course, like all the other boys I knew who were studying musical instruments—violins, clarinets, trumpets, drums—by the time I was 15 I had gone on to other interests. But my musicality was intact; it simply ceased to be so immediately expressive. It was just dumb luck that intervened, as it would again and again, to put me back on the musical track. The first time it happened, the timing wasn't quite right for it. I was working for "Kahn & Shore" and they had assigned me the account of a small record manufacturer. It was a cosmopolitan partnership of four men, a miniature UN. A Jewish guy ran the office. An Italian served as the liaison between the office and the plant where the records were pressed. The plant was run by one German and another guy whose nationality was hard to identify: all I know is that they argued in four languages. I used to take the Hudson Tubes out to their plant in Newark and it was always a kick being there.

At the time the record business was just opening up in terms of

marketing. Up to that point, the contemporary record business consisted of Decca Records and RCA Victor and a couple of other small
labels. Record buyers had a certain loyalty to the major companies
and it was hard for independents to get a toehold. But the new technology that had emerged in the Fifties was making it easier to
record. All of a sudden lots of little record companies began coming
out of the woodwork. Everybody and his uncle cut records.

It wasn't so much that I was conscious of the changes taking
place musically, but I would be in this place, going through files,
making entries, working out balances, and before I knew it, the joint

Sixth Avenue, 1948.

was cooking and grooving–all heads were bobbing up and down to
one of Tico Records' new releases, or one from Seeco Records, or
Eddie Palmieri, Tito Puente, or some other Latin combo, surging out,
hot, hot, hot off the press.

There was always some great piece of new music wafting

through the walls–or at least that's how it felt–catching me unaware as I performed my linear tabulations. Finger-popping blues, early salsa, folk songs from Appalachia. The variety was incredible. One morning I found myself listening to Frankie Lyman and the Teenagers. He had that high plaintive voice, like a rising comet. It was a comet. It was rock-'n-roll. I had never heard of it. No sooner were the copies of Frankie's record pressed and registered on my consciousness, it started eating up the charts.

Music was going through another of its revolutions. This plant, up to that point just a marginal operation, suddenly started to become successful, making money. Making money so fast, in fact, that it was a bit overwhelming. And in the spinoff from that–in the glee of the moment–I was offered a job there as company controller; a real show of faith. I was so flattered; I was just 20. I still had a year of college to complete. The job meant more money–way more–than I could have earned anywhere else at the time. And an opportunity to grow into the music business. Actually, it was terrifying because it was so tempting.

I knew though that if I took the job, my dreams of having my own firm would go up in smoke. Besides, I wanted to learn more about accounting which, as I pictured it, was going to be a great romance. My experience working with Eisner & Lubin, such an important dimension of my business training, still lay ahead of me. I needed to learn and to grow. I might make some money in the short-term, but I'd have had to kiss good-bye the plans I had for the long haul–maybe even passing the CPA exam–because I'd be in some mini-corporate situation. That wasn't what I wanted. So I put the flat-tered feelings in my scrapbook, and kept charging ahead. But that was the first taste I had of what success in the entertainment indus-try could be like.

The experience left me with a taste of reality in another sense, too. Because of the changing fortunes of the business, the Teamsters union tried to organize the plant. At City College we were cutting our teeth on the textbook struggles between labor and management–very functional theories and case studies–but the two sides in Newark were at once a more dynamic and fractional world. I was drawn into the fray, in fact, and appointed an impartial election supervisor. I was so excited about it that I could barely contain myself. This is how 'big business' operates, I said to myself: Pay attention!

The Teamsters, in fact, brought in about 30 people to run their organizing campaign, which was a pretty determined effort, not a simple battle for justice. But apparently they hadn't counted on the management's store of benevolence. The four guys who ran the business believed in treating their workers well; there was nothing the union was promising that they hadn't already provided. The National Labor Relations Board came to the plant and held the election and to the surprise of no one at the company, the union lost the vote.

I don't know what my mother's sense of class struggle would have made of it, but I never saw it as struggle between labor and management. Rather I always saw people struggling to make a success, to make a few bucks, to get on in the world. And I saw that those struggles for success were often more deeply felt and more intensely pursued at an ownership level. I did not see a revolutionary situation. I saw a democratic process unfold, with a simple lesson: in working with people, treat them with the respect due their efforts.

At that point, I thought I had left the music business behind for good: five or six years had passed and Steve and I were traveling another path, it seemed. But in fact, it was a parallel course. The go-between this time was a grandfatherly lawyer, Maxwell T. Cohen. Steve and I had been recommended to Max as a pair of young fellows who could give him the numbers he needed for a business deal he was involved in and he liked how we did it; straight-ahead and fast. I'm not sure how musical Max was, but he was involved in the struggles of the black musician and among his clients were a couple of dozen musicians in the jazz business. He also represented Charlie

Parker's estate.

My only qualm about Max was that he wasn't the most astute guy in the world. He was a good lawyer, but he had his heart where his head should have been. His clients, in my opinion, needed direct,

hands-on management and he, like most attorneys, simply sat back Olympian-like and offered them advice. I don't think he understood the disarray of his clients' financial lives.

Anyway one day he sent over a new client, Nina Simone, so the king of handbags meets a queen of jazz. It is a moment that I would enshrine somehow in my pantheon. For such a meeting, City College hadn't prepared me. Can you prepare for a ride on a roller-coaster? Nina was not only a superb and rare performer, a virtuoso on the piano trained at Julliard, and the high priestess of soul, as the MCs used to say, she was also a volatile lady, subject to manic-depressive swings. Of course, I was a young guy and, where accountancy was concerned, fearless. What did I care if a client had moods? I don't think I even knew the meaning of 'manic-depressive.' Besides it was one of the joys of my young life when Nina was playing downtown at the Village Gate to claim the privileges of working for her and spend an evening watching her perform. Everything that I might have surmised as distancing between us paled in significance compared to the creative energy that Nina poured out. She was female, black and sullen, none of which I could claim to be, yet it was exciting to me to be part of what she was doing.

Probably the thing that made me so sanguine about it all in those days was a high tolerance for eccentricity. In fact, in my compulsiveness to get the job done and to make a success of things, I tended to look right past idiosyncrasies as simply the expression of one's energy. Once I sent a junior accountant out to Nina's home to do payroll taxes. She had a bunch of musicians on her payroll and we had to file these reports quarterly. This was the Sixties; the Civil Rights movement was being radicalized, the Weathermen were at-large, there were riots on campuses. It was all very interesting to me, being liberal and pro-black, pro-Jewish and pro-Puerto Rican. I wanted, and still want, people to be able to get what their work entitles them to. At the time, Nina had a house in a black section of Mt. Vernon, just above Yonkers. Normally, when I wanted to have the job done in a day, I'd go out to her place with the junior accountant who worked for me. On this day, he went out by himself, only to call after an hour or so. Stuttering into the phone, he said "Do you know who is here, up at the house?" He had arrived at the house and at Nina's invitation had gone into the kitchen for lunch to find H. Rap Brown, who the FBI were looking for, at the table. He thought the house was going to be raided at any moment. What should he do?

What should he do? I said, *Be pragmatic! Finish the payroll taxes and come home! Who has time to worry about what's going on with Rap Brown?* Actually, it didn't offend any of my principles of fair play that Nina was involved with Rap Brown. I had nothing against Rap

Brown. He had been charged for inciting violence in struggling for civil rights and was ostensibly a fugitive from justice. But I didn't think of him as a criminal. What to my mind was criminal was depriving people of basic rights. Nor could I conceive of any intellect that would deny a person a place at a public counter for a meal.

Brought up in our own 'ghettos' in the Bronx, I found it easy to identify with the civil rights struggle, even in its infancy. I remember well racial incidents that Nina had on her first road trips, playing clubs around the country, that really upset her. Even though we all anticipated them, that didn't prevent the reality from inflicting its hurt. She and her band would arrive at a place where they had to use a restaurant that barred blacks. The only person the place would actually sell sandwiches to was her sole white musician. It would happen again and again. It rubbed Nina's sensibilities raw and I shared her dismay. By the time Rap Brown materialized in Mt. Vernon, I was working with so many black artists that I felt part of the movement. Doing it by taking care of business, or at least trying to do that. That was part of the struggle, too.

If I succeeded in marshaling the financial aspects of a record deal so that my client got what she or he wanted, it was a building block for the future, theirs and mine. Every concert that went well–not only artistically, but in practical terms–was a milestone in a career. Theirs and mine. In the entertainment business particularly, success built on itself, and to have a hand in keeping it going was incredibly satisfying to me. I felt intimately involved in all of my clients' successes; I was drawn in psychologically. As soon as we began to do business together, I began to dream with them. I didn't just do the books: I listened to what they played, I talked to them about it. I listened to what they said: I didn't just see a client, I saw a teammate. I'd see the decision-making. I'd know in my own mind whether it was right or wrong.

Sometimes the wrong move was all too palpable. At one point, for example, Nina had a big hit with the song, "I Loves You Porgy," from *Porgy and Bess*. Her manager at the time wanted to build on it.

After having reached a certain popularity in the late Fifties and early Sixties, Nina's career for one reason or another had been in eclipse. Now her manager was not only trying to resurrect it, but also trying to take her into the mainstream. The people who were advising her on her recording career were trying to come up with an idea for a follow-up to the hit. The president of the company she was recording for at the time had the brilliant idea of getting Nina to do Duke Ellington's work. It sounded like an exciting possibility to me, both

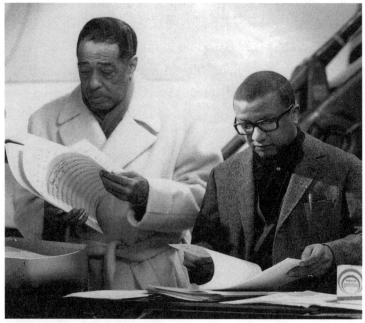

Duke Ellington and Billy Strayhorn.

romantic and musically lush. But Nina must have been in one of her turbulent moods, which closed her off to everything but her own petulance.

"Fuck Duke Ellington," she said imperiously, leaving everybody at a strategy session aghast. That, of course, was a wrong move. For one thing, such vituperation is inappropriate when doing business, no matter how much disdain one might have for the ethics of the business. Maybe it is done that way today, but 30-some years ago, it certainly wasn't kosher. For another thing, artistically it was self-destructive. In fact, later on, Nina did record Ellington's work, and did a wonderful job of it, but the momentum her advisors were try-ing to build on had shifted, and the success that they were after eluded Nina in the end.

I can grow accustomed to roller-coasters, but sometimes with Nina there were hairpin turns that hadn't been there before and they took my breath away. Worse than Dead Man's Curve. She called once to complain that her recording company, which was RCA, was sabo-taging her recording sessions. She felt someone was coming into the studio and either fouling up her tapes, or making sure she couldn't record properly. How this could be I didn't know. There are always problems between record companies and artists and to a great extent artists have a right to feel concerned about their relationships with companies that are blatantly commercial. Most of the time, a record company will make an album and throw it out into the marketplace without making any effort to promote it. If the artist has a certain stature, it will sell x-number of records, but that will be the end of it. So the charge of the company not believing in what it is doing can be sustained. But to feel a record company is sabotaging its own recording session is really going beyond boundaries. I tried to put the situation into perspective for Nina, but it won me no respect.

Later–it was to be our final set-to–Nina felt I was paying the bills of her white creditors before her black creditors. It was at a point when she was neither married nor being managed, and living in a Manhattan apartment that she could neither afford nor justify. The black power movement was picking up steam and the ranks were leaving their white accountants and lawyers and going to black lawyers or black financiers. Which was okay, except that many were incompetent practitioners. Moving just to make a point about color was pitiable, and I had a number of clients who made such moves. In the end, no purpose was served.

Actually, Nina made no such move. But she was becoming increasingly difficult to handle–money wasn't there for her and the type of work she wanted was getting harder to come by. She was allowing herself to be consumed by negatives, one of which was her notion that I was playing racial favorites. It wasn't a violent accusation, but after all we had been through together, it got under my skin. A couple of years earlier, when I was enjoying my first solid success in the business world, and Nina was between managers, I had proposed she let me run her career for a year. Listen to me as if God himself was making pronouncements, I suggested, and success and riches would follow. Maybe it wouldn't happen in a year, I prophesied, but she'd be well on her way. She had looked on my offer uncomprehending: Why would I do that for her? We had been working together on business matters for a dozen years by that point, but on some level she hadn't absorbed the fact that for all that time she had placed her trust in me, and the trust was mutual. She may not have even taken in how much I admired her as an artist. But more to the point, she wasn't sure what to make of the value I placed on her being my first client in show business. She couldn't trust the sentiment that was there. I wanted to repay her for what I felt she did for me. Not that she actually recommended clients. In fact, she begrudged sharing my services with anyone at all. But the fact that she was my client gave me cachet, and all sorts of positive things had followed from it.

Had she been less distracted by her many other priorities, maybe she would have taken my offer more seriously; it wasn't the first or last time I'd be less than convincing. But when Nina accused my office of playing favorites in paying bills, I took personal umbrage. I didn't welcome being a pawn in the culture wars. I knew it was time for change.

Later, alone, I calmed down and found the humor in the situation. What else to do when your heart is broken, or at least feels that way? If I didn't last forever as Nina's business manager, I did outlast three husbands, a handful of managers, and dozens of intense relationships, not to mention streams of club dates and concerts.

That substantially summed up a dozen years of working together, except for one sad and somewhat ironic postscript. Nina had become increasingly drawn into the black separatist movement and for awhile had taken to making strong political pronouncements. At some point, she allegedly made public threats against the U.S. government—it was during the Nixon regime—and the government took an interest in what she was doing.

As part of that period of belligerence, Nina failed to file income tax returns for a couple of years. The Intelligence Section of the IRS was called in: accountants who carry guns. There is nothing more fearful—as anyone who has been in the business knows—than an accountant with a gun. He's liable to fall down and in the process shoot you, as well as himself. For reasons of their own, these fellows took Nina's paranoia quite seriously. And even though Nina couldn't carry out a threat against the corner grocer, these operatives were ready to squelch her. Grand jury proceedings had been started to indict her for tax evasion.

A year later, her new lawyers got in touch with me and wanted to know what my thoughts were about all of this. They were at a loss for what to do. They were already fantasizing a scenario that had Nina behind bars at Sing Sing. The whole thing, from top to bottom, was just unwarranted. This was the singer, Nina Simone, not a mafia chieftain. If her earnings pattern hadn't changed, and she hadn't enjoyed any more success than when she was my client, she was not going to be a serious offender. Get a good tax accountant, I suggested. Reconstruct the tax returns that were not filed. Show the IRS that all she owes is probably not more than $100. File the returns, and if there are penalties pay them. And then call it a day. The advice was my parting pragmatism; my fond farewell. I think Nina's lawyers saw its merits and went with it.

Although I was pragmatic in my business dealings, my point of reference would always be the artist's "greatest good." And that was always a moral question that I didn't take lightly. I took it humorously sometimes, but the humor was always of a profound nature. In fact, I had a chance to laugh a lot and to learn from its source. And sometimes I laughed when I should have been crying.

Meanwhile Maxwell Cohen had apparently thought Steve and I had done such a good job with Nina that he immediately tried to test our mettle again, and referred Ahmad Jamal to us. For awhile in the late Sixties, Ahmad was a god to those who listened to jazz. In my pantheon of greats, Ahmad sits at the piano, forever playing "Poinciana." I still feel nostalgic at the sound of it. But when he came to New York in the early Sixties, his career was floundering and his financial situation was a mess. We were asked to help him with finances and career planning.

Someone with less intelligence would have passed up the business opportunities Ahmad was offered. He wouldn't have been able to understand their complexity, as Ahmad did. But thinking himself a financial guru, Ahmad forged ahead unflinchingly to his detriment.

Ahmad's record label was Chess Records, a small recording company outside of Chicago, Ahmad's home town. When the recording business opened up to independents, Chess was one of the companies that moved into the breach with an extremely stylish sense of the market. When they brought out Ahmad's rendition of "Poinciana," it became wildly popular–all the radio stations played it–and it made Chess and Ahmad a lot of money. Ahmad took his money and invested it in a club in Chicago, where he was the stellar attraction. That in itself was good, except that Ahmad was Muslim and Muslim clubs don't serve liquor, just fruit drinks.

So, ironically, Ahmad had opened a jazz club in Chicago–not too far from where Al Capone used to drink shooters–that not too many people wanted to go to, preferring in that era to listen to their music in a boozier atmosphere. The club, with Ahmad's investment in it, proceeded to go into the toilet. Not only that, but at the time, Ahmad was a prominent star on the nightclub circuit, one who could command fees of $5,000 a week. Not only was his club doing poorly, but by playing there and not somewhere else, he was additionally losing big bucks. Also he had been drawn into some dubious investments by con men. And his house, it was discovered, was structurally unsound, so it couldn't be unloaded. Adding insult to injury, Ahmad was too broke to pay his tax bill and the IRS was on his case. It appeared Chess Records might write him off and let his contract go unrenewed. When he came to New York, he was in bad shape.

When a performer plummets financially, he goes down career-wise, too. His troubles affect work and decision-making. He begins to take undesirable gigs. When the bookers know he needs a job, they offer less than he's worth, and it's a downward spiral. Career success, after all, is largely a matter of perception, whether on top, or in the middle, or inching along. If the bookers see someone coming apart, they back away. If what they see, on the other hand, appears fiscally sound, the opportunities brighten.

So Steve and I gave Ahmad's fiscal persona a dusting, like a first edition that's been on the shelf for awhile. We negotiated with one of the partners at Chess for a new record contract. We made a deal for him with Oscar Cohen of the Associated Booking Corporation, which is one of the big agencies handling jazz artists. We worked with Ahmad in a painstaking way. He had a key to my office, which he was free to use when he needed it. We even partnered on the purchase of some land in upstate New York. There were things he wanted to accomplish and I tried to help him do it.

But again it was the height of the black consciousness movement, and the relationship I was building with Ahmad suddenly shorted out. One day, I came into the office and found all my files relating to Ahmad's business and career interests gone. He had come in during the night or on Sunday and removed my papers, which he felt were his. Everything gone. I got a letter, or was it a phone call, from his new manager, saying that Ahmad didn't want to work with me anymore, and allegations to the effect that we weren't handling his affairs effectively. No mention was made of the $3-4,000 in back fees that he owed us. Just a cool rearrangement of a couple of chess pieces on the board. I understood what was going on, but it didn't make it any more palatable. Paranoia is like acid: it eats into reality until it distorts whatever understanding there is. I always felt some whites were predators of blacks, but I never thought of myself in that category. I'm not sure I've gotten over the feeling of affront, but eventually I was vindicated when years later Ahmad asked me to work with him again, although I passed on it.

Dakota Staton

No less fraught, but more happily Max sent two more clients of his our way: Dakota Staton and Sarah Vaughan. By then Max was thinking of us as his *wunderkinds*, and we were flattered; but these were not the perfect situations we had in mind. Dakota, like Nina Simone, was a great blues and jazz singer, only from an older generation. She and her husband, Caleb Daoud, were Muslim, too. In fact, he had his own storefront mosque in Harlem, which was supported by Dakota's earnings. Now one of the building blocks in creating a tax return is a checking account, even if it is written in hieroglyphics or half-blank. Canceled checks, or deposit slips help to establish some point of reference. But neither Dakota nor Caleb used banks. "People get killed in banks," she said, and she meant it quite seriously. All Dakota had to show me was a box full of paper notations, representing a year's worth of receipts and disbursements: they did everything with cash. Try to put a face on that, Max said blithely. That was a true challenge! We had to scratch around in the dark, until we hit on some of the right questions, and called some promoters. In those instances, Steve was like a rabbi interpreting an obscure passage in the Talmud. If I could resurrect our work with Dakota, I would put it all in my pantheon: the year's worth of chits, the storefront mosque, the club dates that it took to keep everything afloat for that year, the songs Dakota sang, Steve's analytic intuitions.

Even more of a challenge was Sara Vaughan's case, which Max set us up with one Christmas eve in the early Sixties. Sarah, the prima diva of my generation, was at the time married to a football player. They had been living together quite a while, and living on her salary, when she found, she told Max, that this guy was 'stealing' from her. She came to Max with her financial records and asked him to start divorce proceedings. He wanted us to digest everything in her files and in six days come up with a three-year analysis of what went on in this relationship. Except that the Divine One's business records filled six storage boxes. The situation called for an audit *extraordinaire*.

I remember it being a murky night when we picked up the boxes. The whole thing, in fact, was murky and furtive. The lights in our office were the only ones showing anywhere in the area that night, except for the Federal Reserve Bank building across the street. We were working steadily; papers were flying, night turned into day. We were getting the information we needed and putting it together, when Max called on Monday morning.

"Good, morning," Max said. He had called to convey some new information. "This football player, it seems, is upset. He has contacted some hard guys."

Whether that meant hoodlums or what, I wasn't sure, but Max went on. "They're hard guys, and they are coming up to your office to ask for the records. Don't give them anything!"

We had done these jobs before, where we worked day and night in situations, trying to establish ourselves with new clients, and never getting paid a dime. We didn't have to ponder the implications of what Max was imploring us to do. We boxed up all of the 'Vaughan papers,' put them out in the hallway near the elevator, fixed a sign over them, with an arrow indicating what we were referring to, and called Max back to say that if he or his minions arrived before the hard guys, fine; but we were declining the opportunity to pursue the matter further.

Max, of course, threw a fit, but just for a few minutes and then he settled down. Without going too far into Sarah's files we could see that there was no money anywhere, no less enough to steal. The money in question had been blown on good times, and blown by both parties together, living high off the hog. Or at least rather grandly, as befits royalty. But if she wanted some embezzlements as a basis for a divorce, there were a million better ways she could get them.

In the meantime, we connected with John Levy, who managed a lot of jazz artists at the time: "Cannonball' Adderley and his brother Nat, Wes Montgomery, Nancy Wilson, Joe Williams, to name just a few. Levy had started out as a bass player, living the life of playing jazz on the road, and then had moved into the business end of it. We became his accountants and the accountants for John Levy Enterprises. He recommended us to all the jazz artists he handled, if they didn't come to him with someone they were already working with. Without realizing, I became an aficionado of jazz, and the jazz business. When I knew that one of our clients was in town, playing a gig somewhere, or in the recording studio making a record, I'd try to be there. And I'd read the trade papers.

It was a nice market, but nothing great. There were some superstars around, like Louis Armstrong, who made out financially, but basically jazz artists couldn't make a lot of money in the record business, even as late as 1960. Music is all fused now and people will listen to whatever is popular. That was not the case then. In the Sixties, jazz musicians were limited in what they could reach for. The record companies brought out albums and albums were bought by jazz buffs: that was it. A few radio stations had all-jazz programming, but it was hard, if not impossible, to hear jazz outside that milieu. Rarely did you see a jazz artist on the Ed Sullivan Show or on any of the other TV variety programs. Except for Louis Armstrong–but he was also a movie star, in a league by himself–jazz just did not have that kind of appeal. It needed a genius to transform not so much the artists, but the creative possibilities that the artist brought to the situation. How it could be done was demonstrated for us by a record that Wes Montgomery brought out just after we started working with him.

Wes Montgomery

Wes was an incredibly gifted guitarist who played blues in a basic jazz idiom. His record company had teamed him up with a young record producer named Creed Taylor, who was new in the business and which perhaps accounted for the novelty of his approach. He had the idea of using Wes in an instrumental album that would feature mainstream sounds. The album was called 'California Dreaming,' and it became wildly popular. For a moment in time, the money started to happen for Wes. It was particularly satisfying to me because Wes had a large brood of children to support and he was just a wonderful person. I'd catch him sometimes after a set and we'd sit around and talk; each story was a treatise on life. Our only strategy for Wes's good fortune was to help him do some practical things with the money, like setting up insurance policies and the beginnings of a financial plan to protect his family.

Earlier that year, playing in a club engagement, Wes's right hand, which he used to pluck the strings, suddenly froze and stayed frozen, and he had to leave the bandstand. It was an omen, but no one knew at the time. We all just took it as stress, another story of the road.

While I was in California on a business trip a couple of months later, Wes was playing at a club in Los Angeles, so I went out to catch him. Afterwards we talked about what was happening to him and what he might consider doing financially. He was enthusiastic, a new dimension of his life was unfolding. After L.A., he was going home to Indianapolis for a while, and then he was going to come to New York. We would begin to implement all the plans we had discussed.

But he never got to New York. In that two-month period, his health deteriorated and he had a fatal heart attack. After 20 years of being in the business and playing every rat dive, juke joint, and smelly club, his heart gave out. The episode with his hand had been the onset of the illness. After his death, there were some residual royalties, but his family never really got much; finally the royalties dried up. In the end, all that was left was his legend.

So just as there was humor in what Steve and I were doing, lots to laugh at, and wonderful lessons in the social art of ridicule, there was pathos, too. I seldom saw one without the other. It wasn't just on the stage that comedy and tragedy were intertwined. In fact, at one point our office must have been handling business matters for about 15 jazz artists, including Duke Ellington and his band, and that kind of struggle for equilibrium–between critical and financial success–was always an issue. If there was any performer who struggled more for equilibrium than the jazz artist, it was the man, ironically, who played it for laughs.

Just as the handbag scene had opened serendipitously into the jazz scene, the jazz scene, or at least the work we were doing with jazz artists, was the bridge we used to enter the world of professional comedians. By that stage in our work, we felt competent in handling just about anything that the entertainment industry might come calling for. In fact, neither Steve nor I would have been surprised if Falstaff himself had come through the door seeking a plan to fend off the bailiff. Instead it was a funny Italian kid, about my age, who was thinking of turning himself into the IRS, but who thought at the last moment that an accountant might help him sort things out.

Come to think of it, Jackie Vernon, which was a stage name, was a bit Falstaffian. He had Falstaff's predilection for the low road and

Imogene Coca and Sid Caesar.

he had Falstaffian appetites. He just lacked the grandeur. Robert Chartoff had sent him over to us because he hadn't filed his income taxes for a few years. Chartoff was just then in transition to Hollywood. He had a new career in movie production waiting for him, but he was still working as a personal manager, and he had built up a large reputation handling comedic talents–a business he had largely been talked into by his uncle. Chartoff's uncle, Charlie Rapp, belongs in my pantheon, too. He was the booker of acts for hotels in the Borscht Belt, the community of summer resorts in the Catskill mountains 100 miles north of New York City. He had launched the likes of such comic luminaries as Milton Berle, Buddy Hackett, Jerry Lewis and Danny Kaye–people who had contributed as much to my thinking as Adam Smith, if not more. But in the early Sixties, even comic patter was undergoing change, and Charlie couldn't understand a lot of the new guys. If they wanted to fit themselves into something larger than the mountain resort circuit that Charlie understood so well–if they wanted to make more than $150 a night–Charlie couldn't handle them anymore. He was a person who knew his limits. Chartoff had worked for his uncle while he was in law school, and when he graduated Charlie had given him, as a present, Jackie Mason as a client: "Look, I have this comedian. I don't understand his humor. You liked the entertainment business when you worked for me. Why don't you take over his career? Why don't you work with him?" And since Chartoff hadn't really wanted to practice law, why not do this? His mind was made for the job.

By the time I met Bob Chartoff, his personal management company had become Chartoff Winkler Associates (Irwin Winkler was a friend of Bob's and had been an agent) and the comedy acts they handled included Jackie Mason, Stiller & Meara, Charlie Callas, an English group called Hendra & Ollett, and Jackie Vernon. Liking what he knew of my work, Chartoff had taken me on as the firm's accountant. It was a great break–not only for the business it brought Burn & Thau–but because it brought us more squarely into the orbit

of show business. I still had no clear idea of where I was heading, but comedy, like music, was part of my life–for the repartee we engaged in as kids hanging out on the corner in the Bronx, humor was a critical faculty–and getting to rub elbows in that field was akin to getting a shot at playing second base for the New York Giants.

After 20 years of playing joints, doing husband, wife, and mother-in-law

Jackie Vernon

jokes, Jackie Vernon was given an engagement at the Blue Angel. Recognition was coming his way and he had put himself in Bobbie Chartoff's hands. One of the secretaries there had noticed that Jackie hadn't filed a tax return for three years and sent him to see me. Later on, this meeting, somewhat embellished at my expense, became one of Jackie's *shtiks*. I was immortalized and mortified in the same moment, but he and I were made for each other. When I did the numbers and filed his tax returns, he owed the IRS $30, I think. But what he really needed from me, more than any professional skills, was my friendship. And I became very involved. It wasn't very difficult.

I was a newly-wed about this time and feeling very expansive; very grown up and happy, and channeling it all into the business. As far as I was concerned, my wife and my clients were my friends. There wasn't one client I didn't hold out my friendship to. I was open to their bringing me in at any level. And comedians, I found, are so vulnerable to any sign of human affection that when offered it, they could crack your ribs hugging you to their bosoms. Vernon was no exception.

It takes years for a comedian to build up a sense of himself; a sense of where he is going, a sense of his own style. By style, I mean a kind of format that each one learns to follow, no matter who is out there. That's why the Catskills were such a great training ground. These comedians would get up on the stage and tell stupid jokes, and the audiences wouldn't really care. They were at Grossinger's, the most famous resort in the Catskill Mountains—what could be better? They were having a great time. They had themselves to laugh at. Who cared about the comedian? It was a tremendous place to listen and learn.

It was harder in clubs. In a club, when you tell a joke and there is no feedback—only instant rejection—you're naked out there. A musician gets up and plays a piece and even if the audience doesn't like it, there's applause anyway. Jazz artists know they're good; they know they have something even without response. If nothing happens when they play, they simply turn up the amps and play for themselves—consoling themselves with being ahead of their time. The comedian can't be ahead of his time. Neither ahead, nor behind. He has to be right there, of the moment. If he is off just five degrees, he gets zapped. And the rejection is immediate: audiences can fake applause, but it is hard to fake laughter–although I used to be expert at it because I'd go to club dates all the time to support my clients. If wading through that baptism of rejection over and over again for a number of years doesn't make a performer crazy, nothing will.

Up until that time, most people I dealt with were only reasonably unreasonable–people whose demands fell within the norm: their behavior was at least predictable and sometimes understandable. I could work things out. With Jackie, my sympathetic nature was taxed to the max. Deep within, he wanted what I wanted: a family, a nice

Jazz artists know they're good: if nothing happens when they play, they simply turn up the amps and play for themselves.

place to live, the esteem of his fellows and brothers, his aunts and his uncles. But the ante always rose quickly with him. In any one situation, he always took expectations to the edge of lunacy.

He had wonderful material. All comedians develop bits that they're known for and encouraged to do, even though the audience has heard it countless times. Jackie's was about being the dull guy. The dull, gray guy at the bottom of the pile, too stupid even to complain. "At parties," Jackie would quip, "I stayed in the room with the coats." And in fact there were a lot of people around like that in the Fifties, which was a dull, gray time in many respects. Humor, needed in the best of times, was a dire necessity. People needed to have something to laugh at, even if it was themselves, as represented by a comic Everyman. Jackie's dull guy embodied the age. His humor came up from the streets, and there was no performer more streetwise than Jackie. He had wonderful timing, great deadpan, and always put the joke across. He was made for the new medium: television.

He arrived, in fact, just in time to see the TV train pulling into the station: the Dave Garroway Show, the Jack Paar Show, the Steve Allen Show, the Ed Sullivan Show. They all needed comedians. If a performer made it onto one of these shows, and did well there, he achieved instant notoriety. Superstar wages weren't guaranteed, but he would have his pick of club dates, he could pull off a record deal, he could even land a role in a movie. The only drawback about going on TV and doing well was that in five minutes, with a wide viewing audience, he could exhaust material that took five years to develop.

Jackie did well on television: he was part of a new breed of comedians who were storytellers and he could be very funny. His problem was that he wasn't an extemporaneous laughmaker. Everything he did was written down, tried, and tested. He needed to work hard and productively to keep up with the rate of attrition of his material on television. Instead, once he attained some stature, he let his innate laziness get the upper hand. His entire focus at that point was to gain notoriety, cash in on it, and spend the cash as quickly as he got his hands on it. My job was to help him cash in, but also to keep his hands off the cash, except within limits. In Italian, the word limits is *limiti*. It is a word that Jackie never learned from his mother, and consequently never ever learned.

Jackie's propensity to spend more than he made grew the more he made. When he worked on television, there was no problem; I would get the checks. But when he worked clubs, it was another matter. The standard procedure was for the club to pay the agency that booked the date, and for the agency to forward the fee to me minus their percentage. I'd pay the client's personal manager, and travel agent, settle the client's bar bill, and put the balance into the client's account to pay other bills. But at the same time it was axiomatic that the club couldn't be trusted to do anything so simple; clubs couldn't be trusted to stay in business. It was prudent for the client to collect the check at the end of the night: a simple, straight-forward exchange. With Jackie, however, the simple and straight-forward became our continuing game of hide-and-seek. When he returned from an engagement and came into my office, it wasn't a question of having the check; it was how much, if anything, was left. He needed a keeper.

Not only did he spend, he was indiscriminate about what he bought. If his plane was delayed in taking off, he'd wander down to the airport gift shop and buy whatever big or little objects appealed to him, and then he'd go to the luggage shop to buy a fancy leather bag to carry the stuff he bought aboard his plane. When I would object to his impulsiveness–physically object by raising my voice to scream level–he would pull a wristwatch out of his pocket and give it to me, expecting me to be pleased and placated. He must have given me over a dozen during the course of our working together.

One time he came back from San Francisco having spent the entire proceeds of a week at a club called the Hungry Eye–$5,000 on a whole gallery of paintings by an unknown primitive. Actually I'm not sure if primitive is the right word; I might be doing a disservice to a whole genre of artists. The gallery was next door to the Hungry Eye and Jackie could not resist. Not that he knew anything about art. His tastes ran to one-eyed flying horses on beaded mock tapestries.

In Weehauken, where he lived before moving to Manhattan, he and his wife and son had lived in anything but genteel disarray. We drank *vino di Gallo* out of Jewish memorial glasses (candle holders) after the wax had been removed, and didn't think twice about comfort; we made do. Now, living on 57th Street, he had couches and television sets, except there were so many of them that all he had managed to do was create more expensive clutter or chaos. Jackie had lived in such poverty in the years he had to struggle as a performer that when he finally made some money, he just lost himself in conspicuous consumption.

It is a problem with entertainers in general. When they're on top and things are going well, they feel it is always going to go that way, and it is hard to disabuse them of that idea. Not that I really wanted to do that, because confidence is so important to success. In fact, my job was to feed that confidence, trying to help them build an estate. Thus it was often necessary to insulate the artist from the business, especially someone like Jackie Vernon, who was making a good living and doing well, but was not a rock star, rolling in dough.

During this time, Steve and I had about a dozen comedians as clients, all incredibly gifted, all with whom I grew in friendship, laughed with, and cried over, but none who touched me as much as Jackie Vernon. I felt for his struggle for success the way I felt for my own. It was definitely a love; perhaps the love a parent has for a child, even though we were of the same generation. He was so open and honest, and so naive in his handling of money, it could break your heart. If I say he took me to the mat, I mean it was emotionally wrenching to be confronted with such innocence. If he spent all the funds–I used to yell at him–how was I going to keep him alive? It was the human comedy and I was second banana. There is a saying among performers who go out on the road that the show goes on continually, and at various times of the day they let the audience in. That was the way I felt with Jackie.

Once when the funds in his account were really low, he showed up at my office with a Rolls Royce salesman, introduced the man to me, and explained–trying hard to suppress the laughter–that we needed to give the guy $5,000 as a downpayment for the car he wanted to purchase. Jackie knew I couldn't make him appear foolish; he was someone you saw on television: it couldn't be that he had no money. Jackie knew how I felt about keeping up professional images. He enjoyed my discomfort; it was his version of games. *How was Thau going to squirm out of this one?* There was always the mischievous boy in him to contend with.

When Jackie got a four-week booking at the Dunes Hotel in Las Vegas, at $10,000 a week, Steve and I were at once ecstatic for him and, in the next moment, in a panic because of who we were dealing with. We knew that the first week's salary would be given to Jackie as an advance and immediately be consumed by the gaming tables, by drinking and eating, by pals from years of friendship on the road. Jackie's arrival in Las Vegas was a signal for failed comedians and would-be comedy writers to gather. The last week's proceeds were as problematic as the first; Jackie would get his hands on that, too, and between the western desert and the eastern shoreline homeward-bound, he would somehow find ways to consume much of what was there. To salvage at least two of the checks, it was decided I would go out for the middle two weeks and live with Jackie. The engagement included rooms for Jackie's backup organization. He needed a keeper; I would be it.

Of course, I pretended to be on vacation; I didn't want to give Jackie the idea that we didn't trust him. The only trouble was that he forgot to book a room for me, nothing could be had on short notice, and I wound up doubling up with him, which was like checking in to Bedlam. When I arrived, half of humanity was in Jackie's—and my—suite, drinking and eating like tomorrow didn't exist, and the piano player was lying in the pool unnoticed, face up, pissed to the gills. My first thought was, 'Should I be alarmed?' I still had my bags in my hands. My second thought was, 'Who should I be alarmed for?' It didn't take a genius to see that the monies I had come to conserve were quickly being consumed here. My third thought never came. My adrenalines opened and I must have gone berserk. Standing on a chair, I yelled across at Jackie: 'Out!! Get these people out of here!' It was only then that he remembered I was coming. I could tell from the look on his face. I was so mad that for the two weeks I was there, I slept in the bedroom and made Jackie sleep on the couch. He felt too guilty to object.

Actually I recouped in a couple of days and soon enjoyed being there: all I needed was a phone to be in my element, and the nights were full of stars and the smell of the desert. Most of all, I accomplished my mission. But it became clearer and clearer, as time went on, that in certain situations Jackie's innocence was just plain dangerous. He would play clubs run by gangsters and encounter hassles and misunderstandings over money that quickly turned ugly. Then everybody had to run for cover. One time, in Long Island City, where I'd gone to catch Jackie's act, I had to run for the car and drive by the club with the door open so that Jackie could jump in for a getaway as we sped toward the Queensborough Bridge. It was a classic mobster movie scene, except this time it was real. With other incidents, the trouble could be sorted out more easily, but was usually no less consequential. One winter, when Jackie played in the Catskills and invited Dorothy and me to be his guests, the resort owner put us into an unheated bungalow back in the boonies, and it's quite possible that's where our daughter was conceived. It was a matter of either making love all night or freezing to death.

But more problematic was Jackie's mental attitude. We were always behind in paying his bills and I was always nagging him. I took it as a point of pride to be able to meet obligations on time, especially because I felt it made professional sense to do; for one thing, it established credit. But Jackie couldn't treat such considerations seriously. Once on the Johnny Carson Show, he told the story of a creditor who accosted him on the street: "Hey, Jackie! How come I don't get paid? How come I can't get a check from you?" "Look," Jackie says in reply, "once a week I go to see my business manager"and he mentions me by name, which goes out across America via coaxial cable. "We take all the bills and put them in a hat. We take out three bills, and those are the three we pay. If you keep bothering me, this week you're not going into the hat." Exactly how I wanted to be known! But then I laughed, too. This was Damon

Runyon territory, and not to be denied.

At some point, we negotiated a couple of record deals, neither of them enormous successes, but again they were building blocks. Other comedians were going that route and moving into better and better situations; getting access to more well-placed agents. Jackie had a real shot at it because of all the television work he had done. There was a good chance of his moving into acting jobs, if he pushed for it. But after a time, I saw that Jackie wasn't into it, and it became a source of aggravation and frustration for me, which humor didn't dilute anymore. He had reached a certain status in the business, but preferred to stay stuck in the mud and root around in what was familiar and comfortable. The social nature of the business didn't appeal to him. He didn't try to cultivate friendships with the people in the business who befriended him, reaching out for different levels of understanding. Finally, rather abruptly, he decided to go out to California to start anew, and we broke apart.

Even though it was a relief not to have Jackie as my responsibility, I didn't think he was serving his best interests by relocating. The advantages of California had to do with meeting people: more directors, more writers, other artists. Jackie wasn't that kind of a networker or social being. By going out West, he would lose his flexibility to play small clubs and resorts. Compared to the big urban centers on the East coast, California offered slim pickings in that respect to a comic like Jackie. He gave up what he was good at and got little in return. He thought he'd find California easy, but instead he had a bad time of it. His laziness started to take its toll. He lost a chance for a television series because he was physically out of shape. He lost his popularity because his material, which he overused, became dated. Eventually he went bankrupt, and shortly afterward he died, still a youngish man, of a bad heart. The times were a-changing.

Once, at 3 a.m., at the height of our relationship, Jackie called from a hotel somewhere in downtown Manhattan. He needed me to bail him out of a jam—a $100 jam—with a woman he had picked up that evening, and who was now threatening to call the cops unless she was paid for her troubles. I was being plucked from the warm comforts of my wife's bedside and a sound sleep: it was the middle of winter and a bitterly cold night—there were no stars in the sky like in Las Vegas, no moon! Fortunately Dorothy understood these intensities of purpose. This was what a business manager and confidant was sometimes called upon to do, along with tax returns and investment advice.

I expected to be tested by the Jackie Vernons in my business. But more often in this phase of building a practice I just came home beat on Friday night, after five, six days of working nonstop on some project, too exhausted even to have dinner. I'd conk out still wearing my suit and it would take me until 10 p.m. to rouse myself enough to get a bite to eat and change my costume. Then I'd go back to sleep and dream about running through the city. Not in a race, but just running. Running for the physicality of it, the motion, the release. Striding along like the long-distance runner I wanted to be. But, in particular, the dream was about enjoying the place I'm running through, weaving myself into the life there.

5

A Pause in the Running

Dorothy, 1982.

In Aspen, Colorado, which is known in some circles for its floating world of beautiful people on the make, both young and old, it's embarrassing sometimes to be pointed to, by some of our friends, as a standard by which to measure monogamy in its more successful mode. Or, to put it another way, to be pointed out as the anomaly that defines the rule. The secure couple, in Aspen, and everywhere else for that matter, is one of the formative pictures of a good life; belief in 'the couple' is a measure of one's sense of hope. But while I don't deny my good fortune, I can't claim it comes from anything I really understood when I entered the realm. In the beginning I just stumbled into it. I came to understand its values only later on, when I wasn't so enmeshed in what I was doing, or so focused on where I was going that it precluded insight into anything but that. Even when, by some fluke of luck, I captured Dorothy Golden from her life, she had to give me an ultimatum–start a fire under me–before I realized that dating, endless dating, was not the endgame she had in mind. Meeting Dorothy was transformative.

Where it came to the opposite sex, my friends and I had our portraits painted for us by Paddy Chayefsky in his movie, "Marty." Well into our 20s, we hadn't yet figured out a way to talk about the deeper mysteries of sex without getting very self-conscious. We were full of longings, but ill at ease in expressing them. We braced ourselves against those feelings with our busy work lives. During the tax season, I worked two nights a week for Eisner & Lubin, one night a week was given over to doing my duty with the Air National Guard, and the other nights I was either attending classes at Columbia University where I was studying for my Master's in business, or studying for the CPA exam. I don't think I had a free night until I was 26, when Steve and I passed the CPA exams, and we were finally free to shed our schizophrenic work identities. Consequently dating was actually a social ordeal; the one thing that we had on our minds to do with our dates we couldn't talk about.

Dating was for the weekend, never during the week while you were working. To get a date for the weekend, you had to call the girl on Monday or Tuesday. It was an absolutely coded ritual that I found difficult to abide by. Over the phone, you had to make conversation, to participate in social repartee, to chit-chat. I had a weak grasp of the kind of familiarity that was involved. I had no time for such niceties. I much preferred talking about baseball; that I could follow. What I knew about 'relationships' in those days, I could stuff in a picnic hamper. We received no counseling on the subject, either in school or at home.

Actually I longed for a 'steady' relationship, but I didn't want to take the time to deal with the longing. I had very conventional expectations–I was no Casanova. I didn't want to deal with being in a family way. I didn't want to go through the struggling–not until I felt I had enough money in the bank, and knew that I was heading in the right direction.

It was enough for me that I was in these struggles with Fegundio and Vetcher, and Patsy DeMartino, and Harry Haymen, and all our other clients, whose numbers were mounting. I probably had more fun talking to Steve or to my other friends about my clients, reenacting the stories, than going out with the 'gals' I dated. I didn't think I had that much to offer.

Among ourselves, we had a measure of our attractiveness to women. If you were invited in for coffee, it was on the plus side: a symbolic victory. If you kissed while saying goodnight, it was 'Streetcar Named Desire' practically. On some of my dates, I experienced an incredible sense of relief when the date was over. Especially those blind dates. Those could be wicked, for both parties. Sometimes, after taking our dates home, my friends and I would repair for coffee at a Bickford's on the Grand Concourse, or a White Castle on Fordham Road, both of which stayed open into the wee hours of Sunday morning, and testify to our ordeals, convinced that our dates didn't like us, and vice versa.

When I started to date Dorothy, I was 28, which is mature by any standards, but psycho-sexually I was a bit retarded, I think; or at least behind. In my mind, I was still an urchin; I still lived with my

White Castle, Fordham Road.

mother, although I can't say she and I had a home life anymore. I slept on the couch in the living room, where we moved after my father died, and came and went without really discussing things with her. We never had heart-to-heart talks. She never raised questions about my loneliness, or about what I was thinking. In turn, I was remiss about her loneliness and thoughts, which I feel bad about now because there is so much about her I don't know and is lost to me.

After all, she had been a young woman when my father died; in her early 40s, still attractive, with all sorts of ideas, and a passion for Howard Fast's novels, which I inherited. She was for the struggle of the people and I was, too, although as time moved on, my sense of the struggle did too. Thrown back on her own resources again, she went to work as a bookkeeper with Restaurant Associates. Later on, after she'd retired and moved to Florida, I'd send her money from time to time to try to make life easier for her, but instead of spending it on herself, she saved it so that she could leave me something when she died, and so I inherited the money I gave her.

We were both, in our own ways, so traumatized by what had happened to Morris, who was 45 at his death, that we just made an unspoken pact not to get too introspective about each other, although I knew she expected a lot of me. In fact, she held me to a high standard and let me know about it all the time. Her ideal standard comprised two parts 19th-century hopefulness, one part survivor of the Russian revolution, one part American progressive, and one part Jewish moralist.

I remember that just before I met Dorothy, my mother started getting on my case about an affair I was having. Up until that point, my sex life, such as it was, was a non-subject for us. Only once did she allude to it—when she had an uncle of hers come by to talk with me, to my astonishment, about the birds and the bees. Innocent as I might have been, I was way ahead of this guy, just from what I learned from the streets in the Bronx.

My mother felt I was 'behaving badly'. *Trumpernicht!*, she would say decisively, wrapping me on the knuckles with one of a series of Yiddish oaths. All that the affair amounted to was an interlude: a passing fancy. But my mother would deny me even these pleasures. She tried to shame me about it. If I were well-intentioned, I'd be bringing the woman home. I never took her shaming too seriously, and maybe I should have. Maybe I wasn't showing her the respect she wanted. I thought of it as simply the price to be paid for being a guy. I had to withstand her maternal chagrin for months, but I insisted that I knew what I was doing and that when the time came, I would present her with my wife to be; I wouldn't embarrass her. In fact, when that time came for me to introduce Dorothy to her, she kind of spurned Dorothy, and never would give Dorothy her unqualified love like she did our kids.

Dorothy at the time was a school teacher by day and in the

Reaching for the golden ring.

evening a research assistant in the medical library at the Albert Einstein College of Medicine. I suspected that those limpid eyes of hers, which I fell in love with immediately, were on the lookout for Dr. Right. She was dating every young doctor who came around. Fortunately, for me, they were poor, too. There were many miles for them to go still before they could begin to think of settling down, and Dorothy, of course, had that in mind. I was a better prospect. At least, Dorothy saw me as having better prospects. Despite my manner, she encouraged me to go after her.

One of my old friends, one of the New York Indians, and his wife
had made the match. She was going to be my Wednesday night date,
but when I called she said she could only 'do' coffee. The part of the
evening given over to a proper date had already been assigned to
another admirer. But over coffee, I must have passed some test. She
had had enough of blind dates to know that the kingdom of man
was various and sundry; why waste a whole evening. She had it
down to a science. Nevertheless we stayed out most of that evening,
talking a blue streak, spinning webs.The next time we met, we had a
proper date. I picked her up at her house with one of the new T-
birds that Steve and I had bought for ourselves, and she couldn't
resist my panache. She lived in Parkchester, which was a bit upmar-
ket from my part of the Bronx but still modest enough that everyone
came to their window when Dorothy came down to the car to go off
with me. The gossip mills started up immediately. That night we
went dancing at the Copacabana, where Nat King Cole was performing. I knew already that Dorothy was made for me and that I
would have to outdo myself to capture her.

But still my idea was just to go steady. Dorothy became first my
Saturday night date, and then my Wednesday night and Saturday
night date, and then finally my Wednesday, Saturday, and Sunday
date. But that was how I wanted it to be for a while. I didn't really
want to get married. I keenly enjoyed the camaraderie of my friends,
the easy-going banter, the way we laughed at each other, the lies we
told each other. I liked things as they were. I thought I had things
nicely under control. I hadn't understood that love undoes all.

We had wonderful dates. I took her to all my favorite little places:
romantic spots that I'd found in my movements around the city and
had been keeping in reserve for just such a situation. The early ones
were in the Bronx: little Arthur Avenue *restoranté*, Fordham Road
cafés, the RKO Chester, the Burnside theater. Often we'd stop at the
pocket park on Sutton Place to watch the boats going by on the East
River and kiss. Once I took Dorothy to watch the Giants play foot-

ball at the Yankee Stadium. I heard her ask one of her friends, 'What do I wear to a football game?'

We'd often go to see clients of mine at openings–my list in show business was starting to multiply and I wanted to be supportive, even while I was being transformed into a sensualist. Little dives, smoky jazz clubs downtown, comedy clubs in Queens. At the end of the evenings, after smooching for hours on Dorothy's couch, I'd drive home from Parkchester at 3 a.m., always crossing the Bronx by way of Fordham Road, which would be deathly still at that hour. Going by the zoo, the Indians who once hunted and fished in the area would come into my thoughts. In the stillness and darkness, I felt a little like an Indian warrior heading home to the long house, going from couch to couch.

I agonized over a Valentine's Day gift. What kind of chocolate should I send? What kind of message would I be giving? I thought this box would be too big, that one too small. It took me a month to figure out which to choose, taxing my strategic thinking to its limits.

Italian restaurant district on Arthur Avenue in the Bronx during the Depression.

When I finally showed up at Dorothy's apartment that Saturday, it was only to find, to my dismay, 10 other boxes of chocolates tied up in ribbon, and mine was neither the biggest or the smallest. But she acknowledged mine as having special meaning, so I didn't go away defeated. In fact, she sent me a huge valentine that she'd made herself, delivered to my office by messenger. I got the message.

In addition to romance, I was also getting an education in family life. Dorothy's was the only family I saw close up that wasn't dysfunctional. She lived in the midst of what seemed to be like a big extended family, so different from my own situation, which was strictly nuclear in comparison. Her father, George Golden, was a lawyer devoted to public service, and very involved in progressive causes, of which there were many in that time and place. Her mother, Jean, was active, too; among other things, she taught in the children's camp that Dorothy and her sister went to every summer. That part of life I recognized; my parents were also involved in causes. But in Dorothy's household, there was much more *bonhomie* involved. There were always people over, nibbling on cakes, sipping tea, engrossed in their talk–and that was attractive to me. It was like Chekhov. Instead of a cherry orchard that was about to be cut down, the talk was about the Bronx we knew that was starting to undergo enormous changes in a very short period.

In the Thirties, George did his lawyering in New Deal Washington. He worked with Senator Wagner helping to draft the original Social Security legislation. During World War II, he was one of the first lawyers to work on the Office of Price Administration board. Although he never made much money, he was a model, in my mind, of what lawyers should be. He was definitely not the best businessman. He was more interested in getting people together than trading on their problems and prejudices. He should have been working for a major law firm, doing research, drafting legislation, or a law professor. I loved the way he spoke to his children.

He modeled fathering to me, although it would take me a while to achieve the level of sympathetic understanding that he had for his daughters. Certainly he was a lot different from Morris. When he saw that Dorothy and I were heading for the altar, he took me aside and talked to me heart to heart. Dorothy was more like her mom, he said.

These women, he said, have to be kept in high spirits; they tended to run down.

We finally got engaged: I still wasn't making any money, but I could see that I could become successful. My practice with Steve was beginning to take off. Besides, Dorothy had $3,000 in the bank and a teaching license: how wrong could I go? If anything, I thought she might be a little naive for me, Mr. Experience. At a party we went to together, she was offended when someone made a remark that she took for a pass. I thought the guy was paying us a compliment. On the other hand, she had a generous nature and got easily involved with her friends' problems. At first, I saw that as something fraught

Orchard Beach, the Bronx Riviera.

with hassle, but those concerns were short-lived.

More problematic for me–a tiny misgiving–was the threat I felt to my privacy. I could share my privacies with Dorothy, I felt, but I didn't want her mother to have a key to our apartment. Even though I knew it was my insecurity parading itself, I drew the line. There was so much family there in that small household. It was ALL family! Dorothy's mother could well walk into their apartment and open her daughter's mail, which to me was a heinous crime. But that feeling, too, passed as time went on.

Dorothy was just as taken aback with the absence of family on my side. Her story is that she told her mother about it: 'I really like Hal, but there's one thing that bothers me about him. He doesn't have any family!' Dorothy's father, listening in and quick on the uptake said, "It could be a good thing." At least he encouraged his daughter to keep an open mind on the subject.

Anyway, she was the one who decided finally that we should get married. She gave me an ultimatum: it had been a year of dates. Soon I'd be too old for her. She knew I was making moves in that direction, but I wasn't moving fast enough; something was holding me back. My final ploy in favor of delay was to claim physical disability: I needed a hernia operation. At least I thought I did. And I had it in my mind that I couldn't be married until I was physically perfect, shades of Charles Atlas, the perfect specimen. Dorothy laughed loudly and long at the cavil. Okay, she said with great amusement, if I wanted to be perfect, take a few days off and work it out. Afterwards, she said, she'd still be there.

That was actually reassuring. Her logic was unassailable. In fact, my hernia, was a fantasy. A checkup showed no difficulty. In my callow youth, I had had a hernia operation and been told by the doctor that the other side was weak and would probably go. That became transfixed in my mind. It was a slight case of hysteria, not hernia. Over time, I must have strengthened the muscles without realizing it. Angling for a last-minute reprieve, I told the doctor of my concern about being able to carry luggage when Dorothy and I traveled. He said: "Travel light, and carry a lot of money."

The wedding was held at the Concourse Plaza Hotel, up the hill from the Yankee Stadium. Dorothy had organized it all herself. It was the first Sunday in August, when the city is most desolate. When I

Concourse Plaza

woke up that morning, I felt somehow like the last creature on earth. My mother had gone off with Dorothy and her mother to a hairdresser's. They were going to meet me at the hotel later and I was left to fend for myself. Inwood, in upper Manhattan, was not a place where I had friends, so there was no one to meet on the corner on this most significant occasion of my life. Feeling somewhat strange and a little like Chayefsky's 'Marty', I got dressed in my tux and best shoes and went down to the luncheonette on Broadway for bacon and eggs. Sitting on a stool at the counter, I read the sports pages of the *Post*. Then at 12:30, I climbed into the T-bird and drove quietly down the Concourse, thinking about George's dictum about keeping up Dorothy's spirits. I didn't know how I would do that, but I figured it would happen. Everything I passed was so familiar.

I also figured that my clients would shower me with gifts, which would ease the way, but that was a slight misjudgment. After the wedding, we counted the cash and found only enough for a low-budget honeymoon trip to Hawaii, San Francisco, Los Angeles and Disneyland. Still we had fun and when we got back, we moved into an apartment we'd rented on E. 69th Street and Third Ave., anxious to begin working on a life together. It began literally from scratch, particularly for me.

Dorothy was stunned a bit, I think, when I showed up at our apartment with my things from Inwood: a guitar and a little carrying bag with five pairs of underwear that Shirley bought for me, a symbolic transfer of me from her jurisdiction to Dorothy's. "Where are all your possessions?" Dorothy wanted to know. She came with all her high school G.O. books, her diaries, and her hats.

And also, thankfully, with lots of ideas. It was her ideas, and the $3,000 in the bank, that provided the framework for figuring out how to set up house. I could set up a company, but I knew nothing about setting up a household. If you are in the dark, the poet said, move slowly.

Dorothy was teaching in a school in the Bronx, off Bruckner Boulevard, and had to leave the apartment before I did in the morning. So I'd wake up when she did and, for the sheer sensual delight of it, watch her dress. It was a new experience, living with someone who you could do that with, feeling carnal and spiritual about it at the same time. Then I'd get dressed myself, thinking about the things that would have to be dealt with downtown, and off I'd go, purpose personified.

6

Blanchard & Davis

In raising ourselves beyond our modest stations in life, using each other's brains to get a leg up, what Steve and I were doing could end up a disaster! Our enemies could attack, and we could be destroyed! We could lose our Thunderbirds! Who would there be to help us? My father's experience hung over me like a cautionary tale. For years, my mother and I were paying shylocks because of the recklessness of my father's partner. New, underfinanced business partnerships were not for the faint of heart. Like marriages, if you wanted to succeed, not just trip in and out, there were commonplace rules.

Above all, there needed to be a mutual trust. That was bedrock. Two, you needed to understand the nature of the other person's foibles, and be able to accept it. That required at the least tolerance. Thirdly there needed to be grounds for mutual growing—mutual profiting, in the biblical sense. That required a dimension of love, or whatever name you chose for it. Nothing is forever, especially partnerships; but keeping inside those commonplaces substantially lessens the degree of gamble.

Such were my thoughts when I sized up Steve Burn as 'ideal partner' for that first business entity that my life up to that point had prepared me 'to blend into.' For what I had in mind–a business that might eventually lift me above the daily fray and lead into some interesting situations–intuition told me Burn was the best man around. Not only did we instinctively know each other and care about each other because of coming from the same city streets, and the same group of rabbinical interpretations; but Steve was a genius, a mathematical wizard, with a photographic mind. I was smart, too, but it was focused differently. What he came up with as solutions for the problems presented in class were always right on target, and the first to arrive. His intelligence sprang from the gate, mine sauntered. But it was our chemistry that made things happen.

When we first began to do business together, we both assumed responsibility for the ABC's; we did whatever the job called for. But, as the operation grew even minimally complex, Steve took over backstage and I worked the front stage, which reflected a better divide of our basic natures. He liked to be with his thoughts, closing in on the problem, crunching the numbers. My thoughts didn't converge quite so. With me, once an idea is planted, I want to do what I can to bring it to flower, and then to everybody's attention. Steve studied the long-range implications of the tax law and money policy; I managed the day-to-day.

To give our various entrepreneurial schemes some tone, we invented our corporate nomenclature as the situation required. In one operation, I'd be president and he'd be vice president. In another, vice-versa. But our backstage and front stage affinities pretty much held true for much of our 25 years together. In metaphorical terms, I thought of the two of us as Blanchard & Davis.

In the late 1940s, which may have been a more innocent time than now, once the baseball season ended our passion for sports shifted to college football, and no team was followed more avidly in the East Bronx than Army. As far as I remember, we were all Army. Patriotism might have had something to do with it—we had just come out of a war—but the fact is Army was unbeatable then, and we needed to identify with that, and with its stars, who were 'Doc' Blanchard and Glenn Davis.

When you thought about what it took to be All-American, which was a key construct for us, you naturally thought of that pair: Blanchard at fullback, banging through the line of scrimmage off-tackle; Davis at half, taking the ball around the outside. They not only were All-Americans, as I saw it, but without peers as a partnership. I wanted us to be as effective.

Although Steve stands in my pantheon of greats without any question, he wasn't everybody's idea of a favorite son, and sometimes he took even me to the edge of what I could deal with, forc-

Blanchard and Davis.

ing me, like Patrick Henry, to ask for liberty or death. For one thing, his wit was by turns mordant and caustic, which left very little to choose from. And if you didn't 'get it,'–the joke, that is–he would stare you down. It was a form of aggression that he used to telling effect in negotiating sessions, where he could outlast any opponent, but which I didn't enjoy when directed at me. With bulldog tenacity, he would stay at the negotiating table until an agreement was reached. One night, after we had worked on a problem for 12 hours–it was 2 a.m.–I gave up and went home exhausted. He was going to stay behind just to close the office. At 8 a.m., my phone rang; he had stayed up through the night and finished the work. He was waiting in the office, eager to share it with me. Crazy as a loon, or a Bronx eccentric? Maybe there is no difference. During our hippy phase, instead of growing long hair, as I did, Steve wore loud ties and smoked a pipe to express his fellowship in the band of free people.

Joni Mitchell was a client of ours at the time and had moved from New York to California. One tax season, I needed Steve, on a trip to the West Coast, to stop off at Joni's house in Los Angeles and pick up her tax papers. We ran a hands-on accounting practice, as we

Ann Meara and Jerry Stiller, two of our clients, who became good friends.

liked to say; and neither Federal Express nor faxing machines had been invented yet. Joni had kept all of her tax papers together in a drawer where apparently someone, at some point, had left behind a bar of hashish. Steve arrived at Joni's house, emptied the contents of her drawer into his briefcase and caught the first flight back. When I came in to the office in the morning, Joni's papers were sitting on my desk in a neat pile, with the bar of hashish as a paperweight above it. I watched Steve all morning for a sign that it was a joke, but none came. If he thought the hash was mine, he'd turn me in to the police. He had become a lawyer, as well as a CPA, and was very prin-cipled about the law. Of course, if that had been the case, the next day he would have bailed me out; after all, we were partners and best friends. That is how purely he held things.

When we started our partnership, we operated within a purely communist economy: To each according to his needs! Not that either of us could argue the philosophical issues contained in that dictum. But it was a model we endorsed for ourselves. I'm still emotional when I think of the generosity Steve showed me at that point in our lives. He was probably only a bit better off financially than me. When his father died, there was insurance; his mom was left with some-thing, and he had less of a need to contribute to the household than I did. My mother and I had no money. So when our business reached the point of being able to support us both, we each drew about $50 a week, and if there was an extra $50 in the checkbook, I would take it. I needed at least that to support my mother. And Steve never questioned it.

When we started making some money, after a couple of years, I wanted to right the balance. One month we took in an extra $5,000 fee and I wanted him to have it. He was very gallant. For Steve, the thing between us had to be ethically correct or it wasn't correct at all. "What are you talking about, evening things out? Did you put the extra money into a bank account? Did you save it?" He approached the issue of money with talmudic rigor! And I held it the same way. With the rest of humanity, we could be devious; but the partnership was sacrosanct. It was a fundamental precept that we carried for-ward. Eventually, we took the $5,000 and opened a joint savings account. We would do all of those household things together. We even shared an old Lincoln Continental, which proved a real lesson for us in misguided romanticism. Something about the electrical sys-tem was inherently wrong. The generator would burn out every hour of driving. But it was a beautiful-looking machine and whoever needed to go to a client got to use it. Or, whoever had a heavy date; and those decisions were made without effort.

The only trouble was I'd sometimes forget at what curb I parked the car, and Steve would leave it looking like a zoo–which I noticed because I was more meticulous. He left his desk the same way–piled with thousands of papers. Once a month my compulsions would overcome me and I'd be compelled to file away everything I found there. He needed a porter more than a partner.

Occasionally, our tolerance for each other's idiosyncrasies gave out, and we'd scream and holler, until the lawyer across the hall would come running, never knowing when he'd find a double homicide. But at the end of the week, it was us against the world. Two smart New York Indians, shouldering each other's ambitions, trying to break through to the proverbial big-time.

Steve may have been more single-minded in his goals than me. He dreamed of having millions, which is something I couldn't even imagine. His abiding interest then was real estate deals. Now it's race horses. But he trusted my determination, once it had taken shape, to build the practice on the base of all aspects of the entertainment business–even if I couldn't say early on where it would be leading to. In the early Sixties, it happened that the practice was made up essentially of comedians and jazz artists, but by 1963 we started to see a new era forming. You could follow the story month-by-month in Billboard and Variety. Bob Dylan was singing about it: the times, they were a-changing.

A new breed of singer-songwriter was coming forward. The protest against the war in Vietnam had brought them out and was creating a resurgent effect on the folk music business. People like Carole King and Phil Ochs, Dylan and Leonard Cohen, Joni Mitchell. The songs of Jacques Brel. The whole tradition of the European art song. People who were listening were as interested in the poetry as the music. The songs, in many respects, were the poetic expression of the time. The oncoming generation was making a claim for itself, and I was enough of that generation, in emotions, to identify with it. People had had their fill of demagoguery with McCarthy; enough of the Cold War, we wanted out. The artistry of these young performers was becoming the country's conscience and if I wasn't that familiar with the music, neither was I illiterate about it. The work I had done in the jazz field had given me a frame of reference. The imagery was certainly related: personal, intense, contemporary, with the values of everyday life upfront. It was clear that this new music was shaping the commercial market. One of the more innovative periods of American music was being absorbed into the mainstream, and Steve and I let ourselves be taken in with it.

When Chartoff and Winkler went to work in Hollywood, they brought in a young guy named Elliot Roberts to assume some of their managerial obligations in New York. Elliot, in turn, began to bring some of these singers and singing groups into their agency, and refer them on to us for business management, as Chartoff had done with his comedic clients. It started with Joni Mitchell. She was a young Canadian who had been living in Chicago, and singing songs that were mostly autobiographical in coffee houses. Among the songs she had written was one called, "Both Sides Now, or Clouds," which Judy Collins recorded and it had become an enormous hit. The song's success had catapulted Joni onto a much larger stage and she wanted to put herself on solid business footing, so that she would be free to work as an artist and exploit her own creative resources, without being exploited in turn. Her career promised to be big and prolific.

To protect the copyright to her work, we had to set up a publishing company for her. The copyright license, I learned, was the essence of a singer-songwriter's assets. Even if you were starving, you wouldn't want to give it away, as many were talked into doing because they didn't know better. Joni's company was called Siquomb Music. Steve and I put our address on the letterhead and became a small outcropping of the music industry in the heart of the financial district. The curriculum at City College never explored this area in any direct way, but by the early Sixties we had done this work for Duke Ellington, Ahmad Jamal, Nina Simone, and other jazz artists, and we were practiced hands. Joni had a treasure chest of incredible songs and she proceeded to record them on her own, and to enjoy enormous success. Not so much for her voice–which was distinctive enough but not overwhelming–but rather for the way she did her material. She endowed the lyrics with a freshness of feeling that no one else could quite match, and that was being recognized by the listening public. That was true for the whole genre of singer-songwriter compositions.

In one instance during that period, I became not only business manager, but also personal manager of a group called 'The Happenings,' which was another of Elliot's finds. They were four kids from New Jersey, who had begun singing together in high school; Bob Miranda was their lead singer. They took old standards like, "See You in September," "I Got Rhythm," and "Music, Music, Music," and much to the delight of many older song writers and publishers, resurrected them into hits. They added four-part harmony and a new beat and the new sound was wonderful.

Then when Elliot left New York for California, the group was bereft and asked me to help. Although I had never held myself out as a personal manager because I was doing too much other business, I let myself be persuaded. My activism was coming through the closet. I did everything for them from making the bookings to going out on the road and setting up lights and sound.

I'd go out on the road when there were day trips, just to lend my spirit to the enterprise. I remember one engagement early on in a basement bar on Kenmore Square in Boston, 'Ki-ki-ki Katie,' where I had to part two middle-weight bruisers who were about to do damage to each other's faces, so that I could trundle the amps through after a set: "Pardon me, fellows..." Hands-on management, in this case, meant pushing things around, packing up instruments, and quelling the restless natives. I was freshly grown out from my bachelor days, having taken on the mantle of responsible family man, although I could hardly claim to know my Dr. Spock.

For the equipment, we had a truck that a couple of the road guys drove and a couple of cars for the rest of us. Everybody was amused by my wanting to stop every hour to eat, or to relieve myself. They would want to travel in the dark for hours and hours, lost to time. I wanted to treat it as a social occasion. I was on the road!

But after a couple of years, I phased out–The Happenings wasn't happening. The label they were with, appropriately named B.T. Puppy, misunderstood the record business. Though the group had many singles on the charts, B.T. Puppy lacked the operation to distribute and sell their albums properly, and their long-term success never materialized. Meanwhile the program I had laid out with other personal managers was starting to expand and I didn't think they would take kindly to my setting up in competition. I worried I'd lose their patronage.

We were also doing business in this period for four of the main actors in a soap opera on television, which featured a young Donna Mills, who has since achieved successes in evening television and movies. Driving back and forth to Connecticut, I entertained myself with the notion that if I told all of my clients not to show up for work, I could close the soap. I was a potential colossus! Today four actors ; tomorrow the network.

Donna was starting to make real money for the first time in her life and we were helping her deal with it. Then Clint Eastwood asked her to come out to California to be in his film, 'Play Misty for Me," and she needed help to make the decisions. In the entertainment business, young people are asked to make life-shaping decisions with little to go on at the time and having a good support system is critical. She had to decide to have her part in the soap written out, and then go across the country without knowing for sure if the film was going to lead to any other work. But she was a very capable, very organized person, and mostly what I needed to do was just be encouraging.

Elliot also introduced me to the rock n' roll business via Neil Young, who was riding high with enormous success right away. Besides doing his tax work, we helped him buy a lot of property in the San Francisco area. Neil's music was part of a heavier rock scene than I'd known. It taught me basic aspects of the business that I hadn't thought about. It was a faster-moving, more lucrative marketplace, but the problems involved were the same as in jazz. Rock musicians were often treated rudely simply because of the way they looked.

One time, I sent Neil's road manager to the bank to cash a $500 check for expenses. It was lunchtime and nobody was around who knew him. The preppy banker who he was sent to for approval looked at the check, looked at the hair, and said nothing doing. Long hair and dungarees, at that point, were the worst possible calling cards as far as bankers were concerned. What threat it posed, I don't know; I was starting to grow my locks long, too. But since I had just deposited a million dollars in Neil's account, I went in the next day and closed it. I couldn't allow a preppy banker to denigrate my clients. The mores of artists or their employees had to be respected.

Meanwhile, I started working for a club in Greenwich Village called the Bitter End with Fred Weintraub, gentleman-entrepreneur, musical scholar, personal manager. The Bitter End was for folk musicians what the Palace was for burlesque. Once a week, they hosted a giant hootenanny and any ounce of greatness showed itself there. Just about everyone who was considered good in the field played there early on in their careers. Fred brought me in initially to handle the business end of one of the better of the folk groups around, the 'Serendipity Singers,' who operated under his management. When Fred left New York and personal management to get into film production in Hollywood, I became kind of the controller for the club. For that brief spell, I shared responsibility for the place and was there all the time, watching the yeast rise, and the bread bake. I had never seen so many talented young performers in one place before.

While I learned many things in this period, and learned from many people, nothing I learned and no one I learned it from served me more than what I learned from Milt Okun. Milt was the seminal figure in my musical development in this period. Aside from everything else he was good at, he was one of folk music's great teachers. He was a trained classical musician, and loved both the classics and opera, but he had an equal love for folk music, which went back to his boyhood, and an era of social protest, whose stars were Pete Seeger, Burl Ives, Richard Dyer-Bennett, the Weavers, and Josh White.

For awhile he taught music in a public school in Queens, but the school system lost him to the music business for very practical reasons. When he married, he was making $12,000 a year and the prospects of earning more at that point were pretty dim. So he took to the road. His formative years were spent touring with Harry Belafonte, conducting Belafonte's chorus, whose repertoire was Caribbean folk music. And when folk music became the thing, he was one of its leading lights. The advent of the singer-songwriter allowed him to come forward even more influentially.

When we met, he was musical director and record producer for Peter, Paul and Mary, who were then at the height of their careers. He also produced for the Brothers Four and for the Chad Mitchell Trio, both of which were enjoying a substantial success at the time. Chad Mitchell, however, was just at the point of going out on his own and the group was being reorganized. The two remaining singers, Joe Frazier and Mike Kobluk, were moving the group's base from Chicago to New York, and Milt had just hired Chad's replacement, a young singer from L.A. named John Denver, and brought them into the Chartoff-Winkler office for management; I was part of the package. Actually, Milt and I had crossed paths earlier through the jazz artists I worked with, and this second meeting had the hand of fate written all over it.

Milt had a studio in Murray Hill, which he had made into a rehearsal hall, and from time to time, I would go there to talk music with him and to absorb whatever it was he was 'teaching' that day. The first time I came around, in fact, Peter Yarrow, Paul Stookey and Mary Travers were there, working with Milt on new arrangements and they were the biggest thing in the world at that point. It took all of my professional aplomb to keep from asking for their autographs.

To say I watched in fascination is understating it. Milt made us all friends. The studio visits became one of my great pleasures. I liked Milt's thoughtful, understated approach to his work. He had a gift for letting you talk your way out of doing what aesthetically he thought wrong. Under his informal tutelage, my own aesthetic boundaries enlarged. I loved the music he was involved in; I loved the harmonies he arranged. Though he was my senior in years, we had lots in common. He became one of my confidants, and I one of his. And in one of those cracker barrel sessions one day, Milt confided his sense that the young singer he had just hired, John Denver, was possibly a diamond in the rough–polish him and he will sparkle.

Milt had put a call out for Chad's replacement as lead singer of the Mitchell Trio and had received 250 demos from hopefuls around the country, including one from John, who was trying to establish himself on the West Coast. What is extraordinary about Milt's choice is that John's demo wasn't that good. But Milt's ears are precision instruments and he invited John to New York for an audition.

It was John's first visit to New York, and he was traveling with a bad cold. He tried to perform in a style he thought Milt would like, rather than just be himself. He thought the audition had gone poorly for him. Then for two days, he waited for Milt to call back. Milt, in fact, had been dazzled by his performance, and charmed by his vitality and extraordinary energy.

Denver was the son of an Air Force pilot. The twang of his parents' speech was in his voice; they were both Oklahomans. It wasn't quite Will Rogers, who was a favorite figure of John's, but from the same territory, with the same openness of manner. He was, Milt said, almost courtly. He had dropped out of school in Texas the year John Kennedy was killed in Dallas and gone to L.A. to play in the clubs there.

It took Milt about nine days to complete all the auditions and get back to John with the good news. Since the Mitchell trio was essentially going to be a new group and I was going to be the businessman up front, Milt began to share with me what he was thinking. In hindsight, I can see that Milt had recognized in John his *meistersinger*. John revived feelings that Milt had about his calling as a teacher. John's voice at that point wasn't as developed as Chad Mitchell's, but he heard something unique there. Something that wouldn't leave his ear.

He didn't expect that it would make John a star, but it was still something he wanted to nurture in a young singer. The more Milt considered it, the more enthusiastic he let himself be. And Milt wasn't given to hyperbole. He didn't expect the Mitchell Trio to last much longer, but he predicted that John would be a wonder. Wherever music was going, Milt said, it would be worthwhile helping John. Milt was a smart man, and when he talked, I listened. Whenever I could, I'd leave behind all my other obligations for small stretches of time and go out on the road with the trio.

The road, in this case, wound through college campuses and coffee houses. From this remove in time, it strikes a genteel note. Actually, it was a grind. Endless hamburgers in countless Holiday Inns. A hundred gymnasiums to set up in. Places that were hard to reach. On the other hand, the music was great. If you listen to the trio's old albums, you can still hear their unbelievable energy and fabulous harmonies. It was as if they were determined to blow new life into the world singing songs. Milt's repertoire–songs of protest and satire–were songs I liked to sing myself. When I was 10, I was sent to a summer camp in Chicopee, Mass. where somehow I got the idea–which I subsequently tabled–that I was in line to become a Broadway star if I played my cards right. I vaguely remember doing shows, and thinking, 'an actor's life for me.' That fantasy was kind of rekindled here.

And I liked it that John was writing his own songs, as well. That gave the whole enterprise an edge for me. In that period, John wrote what is probably now an American classic, "Leaving on a Jet Plane." It is a song that everyone sings today without necessarily knowing that it came from John's pen. When he wrote it, he was the young artist struggling in anonymity, with the help of his teacher, to master the forms of his craft, just starting to realize his talent.

To manage the trio, we brought in Artie Mogull, one of the great characters of the business, who had the singular talent for judging the fine shades of what artists could and couldn't do. He was really kind of a shark, but a nice shark. Even when he screwed you, he remained likable. After working with him for about a year, he asked me to manage his finances and we got to know each other fairly well. I remember being in a cab with him and saying, 'You know, Artie, I figured you out.' He said, 'What do you mean?' "I really have your number! I know who you are!' He said, 'Well, who am I?' 'You're a guy who makes $50,000 a year and spends $75,000!' 'That's not me, Hal,' he said. 'You don't know me. I'll tell you who I am. I'm a guy who makes $75,000 and spends $100,000.'

A shark with great ears, who always found good people. His secret was that he listened to the lyrics. Whatever he was doing, getting into trouble, getting out of trouble, he was always in the mainstream of something.

The Mitchell Trio started out as imitators of the Kingston Trio. When they first met Milt, they had the Kingston repertoire learned note for note. And as such, they were in that first generation of folk performers who didn't have any tie to the 1930s Depression. The first change in the group was when Joe Frazier joined them. Joe was very radical and pushed the others at least in a political direction, and then Milt came along as their producer and arranger and pushed them even further, injecting the Weavers' songs into their music. Artie booked the dates for the trio and we went after the golden rings.

They were very gifted and very good satirists–good at making fun of things. And when they realized their political material made them unique, they kept at it. Since they were the only people around who were doing this, the best satirical writers in the country were available to write songs for them to perform. Funny, biting, marvelous stuff.

When John came into the group, I don't think he anticipated singing about Nazis in high places and segregation in Mississippi. It wasn't what he was in music to do. He was into rock, and pop, and folk and singing. But he went along with it, and he appreciated it. He didn't talk politics, but he was by that time clear enough in his own

116

beliefs to fight very strongly for the artists' right to express his views. And as time went on, he became more and more imbued with political and social ideas.

Before John came into the group, they were very polished, very smooth, very witty musically. He roughened them up a bit and added

The Mitchell Trio, on tour, the early Sixties.

enormous vitality. He approached the materials as if to say, I'm going to sing this with everything I have, and he brought the other guys out. They were still smoother than anyone else around, but they were also louder, firmer, and a little less contained. They played some wonderful concerts.

But the commercial success we were looking for didn't happen for the group. After about a year and a half, Artie left to work in the recording industry in California and, when we analyzed the figures, we found that the more the group succeeded musically, the more debt it was incurring. It made more sense to disband the Mitchell trio and declare bankruptcy. John, however, objected.

By that time, John and I were becoming close friends. In 1967, when he had married Annie Martell, Dorothy and I had gone out to Minnesota with Joe Frazier and Mike Kobluk to be part of John's family at the wedding. I'd never been in Minnesota: it was Jolly Green Giant country to me. There were more farms than I'd ever seen in one place. That year, in fact, I went to a lot of places that had that same effect on me. Trees, mountains, lakes, roads, cities, towns, villages, the likes of which I'd never seen. Dorothy started a business exchanging vacation homes, and that summer we did an exchange with a family who had a home outside of Geneva near the French border and Annie and John, on tour in Europe with the Mitchell Trio, stayed with us for a week just after their honeymoon. Dorothy and I were older, but we were newly married, too, after a fashion—just a few years earlier our son Michael had been born. We had started to weave our families' lives together.

It was painful to have to tell John about the trio's demise. Even though he was the newest and youngest member of the group, John was one of the most responsible persons I'd ever met. If something had to be done, a car to be rented, or something had to be brought to the stage door, he took it on himself to do. The others took the news of disbanding more matter of factly, like shipyard workers being told they were laid off. Joe was getting ready to enter a Trappist monastery and work with young people who had gotten into trouble with drugs, and Mike was going to spend more time with his growing family and run a music venue. But John was going to stay in the business, and he was dead serious about it all. He was going to team up with new guys and continue to perform. Not only that, he didn't want us to declare bankruptcy for the Mitchell Trio. He intended to pay off the debt himself, which by then was $44,000.

Annie and John, RCA record cover, 'Back Home Again.'

One million people out of 1,000,001 walk away from a thing like that, and never feel obligated. John would have been the last to have any obligation in the matter. Certainly, there was no legal obligation for him. He was never a legal partner of the trio. But he saw it as a matter of honor and he was above all else a man of honor. He had used the trio–he was part of its history–and he wanted to look after its name. It had the same logic for him that later he brought to the idea of being responsible for what happens to planet Earth.

Because he was still going to work with Milt and me on musical projects, he thought of what he was proposing to do in the nature of continuity, which meant a great deal to him. I tried to talk him out of feeling obligated, but I saw it wasn't just a gesture: this was who he was. He had a moral depth that you didn't see often, if ever.

In the beginning, there was nothing to manage, but this Mitchell Trio debt. So along with everything else that was happening in the office, and in my domestic life, I came to have a relationship with a collection agent named Mr. Kolodna. Most of the trio's debt was owed to TWA, but the debt was so old it had gone by the lawyers and had been turned over to a collection agency which, in turn, had assigned the case to Kolodna, as he identified himself to me one morning. He appeared in my office, like an apparition, looking for the Mitchell Trio and raising my hackles:

'You don't see a trio here, do you? This is an office; nobody is singing here! I don't know where they are! They're gone! You want to sue? Sue!'

But Kolodna was not a man to be lightly put off. He called every week for almost a year. John was living with Annie in Minneapolis, and going out on the road with Denver, Boise and Johnson, a new group he had formed, and whenever he had an extra $50 or $100, he'd send it to me and I'd get it to Kolodna. Even though John had a family and was making very little, he was incredibly consistent in whittling away at this thing; he showed great integrity. Kolodna, though, was a hard man to set at ease. He thought the reason he was being paid at all was because of his calls. His calls, he felt, were critical. Once he called my office for an hour straight. And when I'd pick up the phone, he'd hang up. I knew it was him, and I couldn't understand such perversity. Or was it persistence? 'Kolodna,' I had to shout into the phone finally, 'Kolodna, stop doing this!' And the ringing stopped. I could almost see him squeezed into some stuffy phone booth in Grand Central Station and smiling, like the guy who shills for the New York Lottery in television ads, and enjoys being able to move people into states of near panic with the sheer power of his voice.

Once, in a mistaken show of professional courtesy, I told Kolodna a check was coming in momentarily; John had called from the road and he was sending in $100. The next thing I knew Kolodna was sitting in my small outer office, waiting for the mail, and he waited there for six hours.

But finally the debt was worked down to where I felt I could talk Kolodna into a deal. John's star was starting to rise. Peter, Paul & Mary had recorded 'Leaving on a Jet Plane,' and it broke through on the charts. John was being recognized as a talent. Milt had gotten RCA to give John an advance for a series of records.. I offered Kolodna a lump of that advance $5,000, if he got us a waiver from the airline for the rest. They had to forgive $10,000. It was a spurious debt in the first place, as far as I was concerned. Kolodna, to my relief, decided to be reasonable, and took the money. It was the end of our nefarious affair. I never saw him again.

It was also the end of the Sixties. I could tell by the dates on the bills I was writing. For a while, all of these 'entertainment gigs,' my hands-on client obligations–in jazz, in comedy, in folk, in soaps–happened pretty much concurrently. It took the mental acuity of the Ringling Circus lion tamer to manage all the changes demanded–the rearrangement of nuances–in the course of every day or two.

It was still a period of growing and going at it full-tilt. It had been that way the whole decade. But it wasn't the raw struggle anymore, and that pleased me. In that decade, a burden had been lifted. I was learning from a lot of people in every aspect of the entertainment business. I was watching them at their work, watching how they joined hands in deals, watching how they banged heads occasionally: how they comported themselves in the running, as the Victorians in my old neighborhood used to say.

Steve and I were raising families–Michael, a rising *enfant terrible* at PS 6, the public school of choice for the parvenu on the upper East Side, was already giving notice that he would be marching to a different drummer than me; Amy was waiting in the wings (she would become my teacher)and boyhood pals had all but faded into the woodwork. But our hearts, Steve's and mine, still swelled to the idea of the heroic; we still drew on boyhood imagery for inspiration. When we had time on our hands, we used to create models of the way a business manager should operate given the ideal situation. It was our corollary to coming out onto the mound like Sandy Koufax, the ninth inning, the bases loaded, the seventh game of the World Series, and quietly striking out the side.

7

Unpacking Greatness:
The John Denver Story

It was 1968: year of Danny the Red, the Red Brigades, global upheavals. Downtown at 55 Liberty Street, we were trying to bring new ideas to the entrepreneurial side of our interests. Tax seasons had come and gone. Steve and I were no longer hiding from creditors. Our thoughts had turned to the more ethereal problem of creating equity for ourselves. Creating equity is a real test of whether you've imbibed the essential spirit of the capitalistic enterprise, especially when you are trying to do it with no real money of your own. Which is why, along with a vast public, we were watching the market in new stock issues as it swelled daily with possibility.

Companies with new technologies were forming and going public more quickly than you can say Jackie Robinson. Everyone with their wits, however marginal, was investing. The greed factor in the country had made an exponential leap. The investing public rose in the morning with the hope that day of buying stock in the next IBM. Going the rounds was the story about the guy who bought Polaroid at $1 a share, and who was now, of course, a multimillionaire. Forget Onassis, forget Ford, tycoons were going to be a dime a dozen. All you had to know is how to separate the gold from the dross. The market was frothing with activity, moving with two well-placed engines: Technological development and the presence in the country of a lot of money.

The smart investors, of course, jumped in and then quickly jumped out, because the market on a new issue, whatever it was, usually had some rise, if only for the opening hours of trading. What

Steve and I had our eyes open for was the firm whose product was always going to be in fashion, like the lowly widget. Actually, we were working for some of these companies, helping them raise capital.

A lot of them weren't much more than the engineer who had developed the product. The products that came off their drawing boards were actually very good, but the companies and their owner/developer tended to be poor at merchandising, poor managers, and undercapitalized. The most important ingredient in dealing with this situation was getting financing, and going public was one of the best ways to do that. If one of our clients had a good six months of earnings, we'd encourage them to try. If you could show that your product had a chance of claiming a niche in the marketplace, you wouldn't have too much trouble raising the capital you needed.

The expression for an undercapitalized company in those days for us was 'either go public or bankrupt.' Going public meant giving up a share of ownership, but if the investors were a diversified lot, there was little danger of an owner losing control. You could give away as much as 50 percent or more of the company and still control its destiny.

We were dealing with small financial underwriters at the time, including one which we called the "court of last resort," and our motto was, 'If he would not do your deal, it was not doable.' From this point in time, it all seems more dreamlike than real. I remember a situation where, for three hours, we were discussing taking a client public, dissecting the firm's financial position, trying to devise the right ratios to establish a proper offering price, when the principal owner of the brokerage house signaled an end to the discussion by stating, "I don't care what you guys have come up with, the offering price is going to be $5 a share, not $3. I make more money that way." So much for the finer shadings of our emerging financial acumen. For a moment, I felt myself back in Jennings Street market, in the Bronx, watching the old housewives haggling for eggs and day-old bread.

We were active players here, but earning only fees, not building equity. Accountants were forbidden by the rules of the Securities & Exchange Commission to own stock in publicly held companies for which they certified financial statements. If they owned stock, how

Companies came and went like clouds in the sky.

could they be impartial? So, we had to figure out something else. Why not package, we philosophized, what we already knew, and go public ourselves? The technologies that were powering the market were transforming the music industry, as well. Why not ride those possibilities?

One thing that we had become very good at was auditing record companies' books of account to see that our recording artists were paid the right amount of royalties. Another company, the Harry Fox Agency, did this work, too, but only for music publishers. No commercial company offered that service to recording artists and record producers. Each artist was left solo, along with his or her agent, lawyer, or accountant, to see to it that he or she got the correct royalty count. And getting the right count was not easy; it still isn't. It's not the straightforward affair some pretend it to be. Record contracts, like movie contracts, are complicated instruments. An artist can be ruined financially if he or she is mishandled. Even after everyone involved seems to agree to its terms, disputes arise constantly. A written agreement still leaves room for interpretation. Recording artists and record producers are robbed blind and the record companies get away with it.

Plus there is the fact that record companies withhold a big chunk of the royalties for a long time before they part with it. Say a record comes out in September and becomes a big hit immediately: a lot of money begins to accumulate. The record companies aren't anxious to redistribute any of that too quickly. You'd get a royalty statement in December, a royalty payment in February of the next year, and then further payments, if any, only every six months thereafter. And on the way to the forum, numbers get lost, or skewed.

Our idea, simply, was to form an organization to audit record companies on behalf of artists and producers. For that service, we'd charge a retainer and a fee based on a percentage of recovery. If the record company sent an artist a check for $200,000 and we found that the proper payment should have been $300,000, we'd get a percentage of the additional $100,000 recovered. The theory was that since there weren't a great many record companies, the most efficient approach for us would be to sign artists in clumps: a dozen from one record company, a dozen from another, and so on. We'd profit and they'd profit. Every knowledgeable person I raised the idea with agreed it had enormous possibility. All it needed was a little cooperation from artists, their agents, their lawyers, managers, producers—in other words, most of the people who made up the record business. I had an easier time trying to find a parking space in midtown Manhattan on Saturday night.

Once we announced our intention to seek "public financing" for a new auditing company we were calling Royalty Controls Corporation, the Attorney General's office of New York State came after us. An accounting firm working for the Harry Fox Agency, in their infinite paranoia about our being competitors, misread our statement of purpose and accused us of being professionally unethical. They were dubious about what we were doing and thought we would put them out of business. We pushed legal papers back and forth with the attorney general's office until it seemed like the process would never end.

It took a year, but we persevered. And by going public, we had raised $300,000: I was like a boy with a new toy. A toy even better than a cheese box bank. We put the money in CDs at 10 percent interest and–wave of the magic wand–we could already count on $30,000 in yearly interest. In my prayers at night, I evoked the gods of City College and thanked them for showing me the path. I also lit a candle at St. Patrick's as a way of thanking the city for taking care of me at a certain level of nurturance. I could feel the demons of insecurity in my gut decamping.

Of course, we couldn't just do anything with the company's money. When you were a public company, rules come into play. You have to file reports with the Securities & Exchange Commission. You have to account for the way you spend investors' money. One could squander the money, paying out big salaries, as many firms do, and fail because of that; but that wasn't our game. We wanted to leverage our assets and buy other companies. The idea was to control the money, not to take it.

Our board of directors, which was made up of clients and friends, whose shades I would install as an ensemble on the second floor of my pantheon, represented by notes from the meetings which were attended mostly by Steve and myself, included Duke Ellington, Jerry Stiller, Skitch Henderson, Burl Ives, Joni Mitchell, Nina Simone, Tom Paxton, Julian "Cannonball" Adderley, Jane Morgan and Jackie Vernon. I was president and Steve was the vice president. Where could investors find a more glamorous depository for their tertiary funds? We were show business!!

In fact, no sooner had our common shares been issued than they were selling for $5 a share, and then in a month it was up to $10.

Our underwriter was talking the company up, trying to make the shares more attractive–notoriety that I wasn't eager to have quite then. We did have a great idea, we were good managers and merchandisers, and we got things done; but we were just starting out. I wasn't looking to fool investors.

Julian 'Cannonball' Adderley, one of our board members

When the stock reached $10, a cousin-in-law of mine, who was always checking on the state of my capital accumulation, came running up to my office with the news that I was worth a million dollars! I could have done without his attentions at that point, but we hugged each other and danced around. What else could I do? I couldn't be rude.

Of course, when the market collapsed a few months later and the stock plummeted to $3, my cousin-in-law returned with the news that I had been wiped out! "You've just lost $700,000! You're not rich anymore!" There were no words of consolation.

Actually, Steve and I had been having new thoughts all along about what we were doing. The market had collapsed? Okay! Our underwriters were out of business? Okay! In fact, it had become increasingly clear that other accountants and lawyers were resisting what Royalty Controls was offering. There was fear we would steal their clients. The ground for what we proposed had shifted. The idea was right, it just wasn't the right time for us any more.

On the other hand, we still had a viable company, a publicly held company, and a great deal of money to operate with. We had a wonderful list of clients in the entertainment business who were doing well. The industry was prospering like nothing else in the country. The new technologies had been transformative. So instead of dissolving Royalty Controls and distributing its funds, we decided to shift the focus of the company to business management, specializing in the entertainment industry.

Milt, on a parallel course, had meanwhile been bringing John Denver along musically. The folk era had ended and Milt had moved to London to take life at a more leisurely pace, but he would return

Milt Okun

to Manhattan a couple times a year to work in his studio with a handful of artists, and these included John, who was now signed to a record contract with RCA.

Fifteen record companies had turned down John's tapes, but on Milt's 16th try Harry Jenkins, the executive at RCA who had signed Elvis Presley, liked what he heard. John was in town one day and Milt arranged for him to meet Jenkins and sing for him. Jenkins was charmed and offered Milt a contract on the spot. Milt, in fact, had been unprepared for such a fast turnaround. When Harry asked about the kind of advance he was looking for, Milt had to come up with a figure very quickly.

"Twenty thousand," Milt had blurted out.

"Twenty thousand?" Harry had looked a little surprised. It was a lot for a first record. "Oh!" Milt said, trying to recover, "That's for four records."

"Twenty thousand for four records," Harry said, looking more comprehending, "That seems quite manageable. I'll send you a contract in the mail."

Usually record companies guaranteed no more than two recordings, especially for someone just starting out. Why $20,000 and why the number four to bring Jenkins along? It was like a stone thrown into a still pond because it was only on that fourth album that John broke through.

I didn't exactly hang out at recording sessions, but I tried to listen to what was going on in different phases. First I'd listen to the unmixed versions, where I could hear the musicianship and the vocals in their most pristine state; I'd come down to the studio to watch and listen and be part of it. The first three recordings John made, I thought, had as much good music on them as the fourth one did, and at least a half dozen songs that sounded like hits in the studio. But what went on in the studio, I learned, was not the only determinant of what went on in the marketplace.

John was really into his game in the studio. Some artists spend months there, getting it right. He could do an album in two to three weeks. The first stage would be John alone, coming in to do a reference track. He'd sing all the songs on the album—just the basic guitar arrangements. Then the musicians would come in and lay down the music tracks, which was a big aspect of the album. Then John would return and vocalize to the new tracks. Finally, if they were needed, "sweeteners" would be brought in; an orchestra on one track, a bongo drum on another, etc. When all these steps were completed, John and Milt would sit down with the engineers and do a mix, the crucial blending of the different sounds together into a final product. All the early phases could work and an artist could still "lose the record" if the mix didn't go right.

In the early phases of recording, Dorothy would ask in the morning: "Were those the new lyrics I heard last night?" I apparently sang in my sleep. I did all I could to keep my mind on other business that needed attending, but what I'd hear at the studio would play on in my head until it was safely pressed into the final product. Even though I was nominally just a bystander in the process, I lived it as intensely as all the others.

The fact is, I was less a bystander than a silent partner, but my coming down to the studio had to do with wanting to be a part of the creative process, and not simply assuming an obligation to one's partner or friend. If something was going to happen—if the magic was going to manifest itself—I wanted to be in on it. That was always the nature of the game for me.

Once Royalty Controls was firmly established as a business management company, we sold the assets of our accounting practice. Steve went off to Florida to pursue deals in real estate, and I moved our offices uptown to 10 Columbus Circle, the same building that housed the corporate offices of the New York football Giants. I knew the boy in me still lived when my first thought on seeing their nameplate on the door was for the autographs I might get. Dorothy, on the other hand, burst into tears when she came up to see the modest setup. The thought of my starting all over was too much for her to bear.

It was like starting over for me, too, except that instead of wanting to cry about it, I felt like running over the rooftops of the city. At the recording studio, neither of my partners, Milt and John, needed help with the music from me, but they wanted to know how I felt about it: we were a team. What did I think? How did it sound? Was I enjoying it? Where were we going?

In the first couple of recordings of the deal with RCA, Milt had

John stay conceptually close to the folk scene. John recorded some of his own songs, but Milt was still essentially focusing on John as a performer, not as a writer. The albums were produced with the idea that we were supporting the career of a folk singer as he was developing his sound. In the first album "Rhymes and Reasons," he did the song, "Leaving on a Jet Plane." Few recognized it as the great song it is until Milt had Peter, Paul, & Mary record it a year later. None of the first three albums had songs that became commercial hits. On the other hand, the albums did reasonably well. I was happy with what was happening, and so was John.

After his third album, 'Whose Garden Was This?' he was getting better dates, making more money, and attracting more industry attention. It felt like the right time to invest in a personal manager for him—someone who could stay on top of things as they developed on a daily basis. I suggested a promoter-manager named Jerry Weintraub, who at the time was Jackie Vernon's personal manager, and a promoter with a great deal of experience behind him. He had done nothing I would call notable at that point, but he was the classic go-getter. More to the point, he was also handling an act called Zager and Evans, which had just recorded a big hit for RCA. It is a fast-paced business. There are many agents and managers trying to move their clients along. The record companies were always getting distracted. When they saw an artist could deliver the "Big One," they'd try to stay focused with you. As an RCA recording artist, John needed someone not only to help him develop as a performer, but to push RCA's hand into doing things for his recording career. Jerry seemed made for the job.

It wouldn't occur to me until later that what I'd let myself be enthralled by was the figure of "Sammy Glick" incarnate, the anti-hero of the Budd Schulberg novel, "What Makes Sammy Run." The wise guy posturing should have warned me off. But then I was no stranger to such postures; we were boys of the same city. I read it as an affectation rather than the incipient megalomania that it really was.

Nor was I all that sure John and Jerry would get along for more than five minutes. Temperamentally they were from different constellations. At their first meeting, they looked as if they both had been sent by central casting: John in summer sandals and a guitar

One corner of Broadway and W. 47th Street, spiritual home of the classic Broadway go-getter. 1936. It was then and there that the archetype fast-talking, wise-guy posturing New York promoter-manager germinated and grew new edges. Professionally this, as much as anything, was Jerry's native ground. The biggest bargain in town was the Burlesk show at the Central Theater, which had fallen on hard times. Seats were only 25 cents. And 'Hold Your Horses' was playing at the Winter Garden.

slung over his back; Jerry in a sharkskin suit, the archetype fast-talking New York manager. But again it was the chemistry that interested me. I thought pairing the two might produce the desired effect.

Six months later, John's fourth album, 'Poems, Prayers and Promises,' broke on the charts and we were beyond ruminating about where, when and how it would happen. After the sale of the single, 'Take Me Home, Country Roads,' started to push through the top, I felt a little like Redd Fox on television, when he grabs his chest and pretends his heart is giving out: 'This is the Big One!' John came forward on that recording with a clear sense of his own aesthetic, Milt was the teacher wise enough to encourage it, and Jerry's bravado, thinking and sense of showmanship inspired RCA to put extra effort into promoting the work.

By then, it was clearly the case that what John was writing weren't just pretty pop songs, but expressing in song something essentially true about America, which was a matter of interest, as it turned out, to millions of other people. The songs on 'Poems' expressed all the themes that John would pursue for the next 10 years: 'Take Me Home, Country Roads,' a song that John had just written with Bill and Taffy Danoff, when they were performing together at the Cellar Door in Washington, DC.; 'Sunshine on My Shoulders;' the James Taylor hit, 'Fire and Rain;' a poem called 'The Box,' a parable about the moral issues involved in deciding whether to keep war in the box, or to let it out; the Beatles' stirring anthem, 'Let It Be;' the Danoff's song, 'Gospel Changes;' a song of John's called 'My Sweet Lady,' and another called 'I'd Rather Be in Colorado,' where he was starting to explore his love for the mountains and the majesty of the physical world. They were the themes that defined the artist, but they managed at the same time to convey longings that were felt all over this land.

John, in his modesty, told people Jerry had rented storerooms all over the country and that it was he who was buying his records and storing them there to make him look good.

Then in the fall of 1972, after a fifth album called 'Aerie,' which was a disappointment commercially despite the good work on it, John recorded 'Rocky Mountain High,' his love song to the mountains (which was also John's farewell tribute to a compatriot of his who had just died tragically in a motorcycle accident), and that song swept the country. After that, no one could avoid recognizing the name of John Denver. After that, recording success for John became a common phenomenon. It created for him an enormous following. For the next five years, going around with John would be like being with the heavyweight champion. Everyone wanted to book him; every arena wanted him on their schedule. He crossed over from 'rising young folk singer' to popular icon.

In London–in 1973–where he had gone to work in television at Jerry's impetus, John set up shop in the studios at Shepherd's Bush Green and for a couple of months did a variety show that the English devoured, and from which he learned a new craft, which he was exceedingly good at. At the same time, the earlier releases–'Poems, Prayers and Promises' and 'Rhymes and Reasons'–started to make their way up the UK charts. It was really his start as an international artist. Concerts in other European cities followed. That fall, he recorded his first 'Greatest Hits' album and it became the largest

With John and his brother Ron Deutschendorf.

selling album ever put out by the RCA organization.

And then no sooner had we digested that success than the single recording of 'Sunshine On My Shoulders' rose to Number One on the charts, followed soon by the success of 'Annie's Song,' and then 'Back Home Again.' Wherever you turned, John's work was being played. The music, in fact, had become more than itself. People were finding all kinds of transcendent meanings. In one instance, one of John's songs was given star billing in a made-for-TV movie aired on one of the major networks. The movie, appropriately called 'Sunshine on My Shoulders,' was based on a story that had appeared first in the daily press about a woman dying of cancer. The song's inspirational qualities are incorporated not just as background, but as part of the central movement of the drama, which of course gave John additional notoriety. People were having his songs sung at weddings, at funerals, at *bar mitzvahs*, at church fellowships, at bridge openings, at ship launchings.

It was a cultural phenomenon; someone less modest than John would have had his sense of reality distorted by it. Not that his wasn't, but a moral imagination kept him this side of the abyss, where celebrity carries you off. The work he had done with the Mitchell Trio had been politicizing. He may not have known then how it would play out, but passionate feelings about contributing to public life had been nourished, and suddenly his popularity had given him license to explore this. In addition, it was no small thing for him that he came from a family that, on both sides, had known what it was like to be disenfranchised. Their experience had registered with John at an early age. He was very much in touch with it and drawn toward it. Finding simple statements to articulate his convictions, John vocalized in song particular feelings that no one else was dealing with. In his own way, he became a spokesman for the age.

I found the English the most perceptive about John's work–maybe because they could be objective. In the April 30, 1975 issue of *Melody Maker*, Ray Coleman began his review of John's British debut at the Palladium (2,300 seats on each of eight nights, sold out in 10 hours) with unabashed approval:

An American friend, the great and tragically neglected singer John Stewart, said to me four years ago: "Watch John Denver.

He's a genius. He'll defeat all the cynicism in the world because he's so real. You don't have to think too much about him—just lie back and let his sunshine wash all over you. And you know, you'll feel real."

These words have rung in my ears for years, as the Denver story unfolded to its current mind-boggling height: The tall Texan was one of the world's biggest box office and record attractions.

At the London Palladium where he opened that Monday for five sellout nights, (15,000) tickets were as valuable as gold.

Denver still touches the nerve of those who still want to believe that dreams can be achieved wherever we live.

John Stewart, of course, had been the lead singer with the Kingston Trio and for a brief time he and John had teamed up and performed together.

Nevertheless, much of the U. S. pop music intelligentsia derided John. They distrusted his plain words. They thought the songs simplistic, or too optimistic. They couldn't understand why his music was so successful, why his concerts were always sold out. Why his television shows were watched by millions. Most of the music critics at the time had grown up with a heavy metal music sound reverberating in their ears. Although it was always hard in those circumstances to get air time for John's music, when radio stations played his records audiences responded.

By 1975, John was the number one recording artist in the country in terms of records sold. His audience was huge and diverse. After his stint on English television, ABC signed John to a series of 12 musical variety specials—two a year for six years. We formed our own production company: JohnJer Productions, with John, Jerry,

Milt, and myself as principles. That summer, John made his cabaret debut at Harrah's Casino in Lake Tahoe, co-heading a show with Frank Sinatra that broke all the house records for attendance. At the same time, the Country Music Association named John Entertainer of the Year. His song "Back Home Again" was named by CMA as song of the year. He also won an Emmy award for his television special, "An Evening with John Denver." The honors unfurled. One

By 1975, the Denver tour's road crew numbered more than 30 people. It was like touring with a ball club. In fact, for a while it was suspected that John's road manager would hire musicians only if they had something to add to our softball team.

observer of the pop life said, "What Sinatra was to the 40's, Presley to the 50's and the Beatles to the 60's, Denver is to the 70's–a phenomenon."

For me, there was no question: I had apprehended a fantasy. It wasn't just that I started to enjoy financial success. It was something more fulfilling; I'd helped give shape to John's success. The recognition that was bestowed on him was bestowed on me, too. The hits.

Song of the Year. Performer of the Year. The public exposure. It was all happening to me, too, just in another register. And I needed to ground it in something of my own making. Not quite then; I wasn't stopping to analyze my dreams. When you're on top, you don't stop to think about the changes taking place. You just go on to the next thing. If you want to stay up there–and I did, for as long as I could–you have to bring more coals to the fire, more than you brought in the first place. But I let myself dream on.

Occasionally my intensity would get the better of me. If we paid good money for something to happen and it didn't happen, whether it cost $5 or $5,000, I'd want to retaliate. John was more spiritual about these things. He would tell me to let it go. If I had the fore-sight to see how big John was going to become, perhaps I would have let go sooner. I had a long list of clients whose business affairs I was still taking care of and every client relationship–every business relationship, for that matter–brought with it another layer of intensi-ty. So while the new thoughts crowded in, and my ambitions were shifting, I tended not to be such a free spirit.

With the success of "Rocky Mountain High," John had given us a free hand in building his estate, and I started to put in a lot of miles traveling on his behalf. When I wanted to talk with him, the best way to do it was to catch up with him on the road. Life on the road, I found, was an endless tapestry, and got more and more complicated as time passed. In the early years of touring, John went out with only a couple of musicians and a road manager. When he could afford Kris O'Connor, an old friend from the Cellar Door, to be his full time road manager, it was a real milestone. By 1975, the tour encom-passed a crew of more than 30 people which included front stage, backstage, transportation and other support personnel. It was a real spectacle that essentially had to be reinvented each time: Where it went, how it went, who went with it. It helped to know first-hand the places and people involved. And of course I got to mix business and pleasure. It was like touring with a ball club. In fact, for a while it was suspected that John's road manager would hire personnel for the crew only if they were a good addition to our softball team.

I remember playing one softball game where I think my job was on the line. I was never the greatest softball player, but I was motivated. It was the eighth inning. There were people on base, we were leading by one run. I was in right field. The ball was hit almost to the fence. Somehow, I got back there, and made an over-the-shoulder catch. It worries me sometimes to speculate that if I hadn't made the catch, my career might have taken a different turn.

I was like the good executive who owns an oil rig and gets down and starts drilling with the drillers. I wanted to understand what the problems were, and what the possibilities were, and what everybody's feelings were. I wanted to understand directly from the situation that if you are on tour, traveling by bus, you shouldn't go more than 300 miles in a day. It is something you needed to think about when you were setting up a tour. I wanted to *feel* the thing, not just know it economically or statistically.

I viscerally needed to feel the crowd. Feel it when the lights would come up, the sound would spill in, the stage would fill. I was always moved by the spirit of the thing. I could see the audiences, the different faces, their attentiveness when John was on stage. The same yearning that would fly out of them, and upwards, when John sang about the Rockies, or about Annie, or about Uncle Matthew losing his farm.

I have a vivid memory of this one family—a farmer and his wife, and their three children—sitting right up front, never taking their eyes from John the whole time he was performing; they gave the word enraptured a new meaning. We were playing a concert in the Midwest and it was during a recession year in the farm belt. Afterwards, John said: "Did you see that family? Do you know how much money it took for them to come to see me? I know they didn't have much money." John said he was singing to them all night.

The scenarios were always changing. Dozens of towns, large and small. Dozens of special needs. Sometimes Weintraub would show up, going on about the size of his room, or the size of his bed. It annoyed him not to be able to get a king-sized bed; for things not to be the way he wanted them. The saving grace was that he didn't stay long. He traveled his own routes.

On the European tour in 1979, I was the official money changer: The Bank of Thau. I went from place to place with a briefcase full of Euro-currencies. I was seeing Europe for the first time. Dorothy and I had lived outside Geneva one summer, but we hadn't really toured Europe. In Paris, we stayed at the Maurice, where the Nazi high command set up their headquarters in WWII; talk about auras. Everyone had double rooms. Dorothy came from Connecticut and Annie came from Aspen. We never made much money on foreign tours, but we lived well; which was part of John's basic ethic: John's band and support personnel always stayed at the same hotels as he did, which was uncommon in the business. What he did for himself, he did for others.

While the songs, from place to place, may have been the same, and the style of the show the same as the one before, each audience and each concert were different. Equally for me, each time I went into a new arena, a new city, it was a fresh experience. A new set of people to meet–people to whom I may have spoken or written; maybe the guy who booked the show; a new welcome to absorb. John's reputation preceded him; everywhere he went he was showered with affection, which washed off on those of us who traveled with him. Afterwards, after the concerts, there'd be a dinner at some restaurant. Or if a movie was playing in town that everyone wanted to see, John would rent the theater after their last show, and we'd usher in the morning there. They would even open their popcorn machine for us and, of course, John supplied the champagne. Popcorn, champagne, and a good movie: It was a great life.

When my son, Michael, got a little older, I sometimes took him along on tour. He started playing the guitar and had become a devoteè of Eric Clapton. His musical tastes ranged on the wilder side of where we were, but he loved John's concerts. I think he also enjoyed the social life it afforded him. I remember him one night after a show, after he had turned 16. I had dropped by the hospitality room at our hotel to see what was happening, and there he was with the crew, the ladies, and the booze, coming on like a man of the world. When I tried to grab Michael and head him back to the fold, I was shouted down by the others, all of whom were crazed by then. I knew he was precocious, but I wasn't prepared to see it. I didn't

At Ground Zero, Hiroshima, with Tom Crum and John.

think his mother would be pleased to hear of this.

Meanwhile that sacker of cities, Jerry Weintraub, who had been slouching his way toward Malibu, had entered the city. The empire was building; the sacks were filling. Driving everything ahead of him with his will, spreading his influence with great fanfare, he was rising on John's popularity to his own place of prominence in a powerful industry. One had to admire the man's audacity. We were experiencing the apotheosis of a Hollywood mogul!

In 1975, the year John was the industry's top earner, Weintraub won recognition in Hollywood from the B'Nai Br'ith in Los Angeles as Man of the Year. The occasion marking it was a gala at the Beverly

Hilton in Hollywood and all the big stars came out. The entertainment that night was Frank Sinatra, Diana Ross, and John Denver. And, for good measure, the speakers were Henry Kissinger, and Itzhak Rabin, Prime Minister of Israel. If I didn't know Jerry, it would have all been convincing.

Looking back on that evening, what's interesting about it to me is how indifferent Jerry already was to what was going on that evening. While he worked the crowd–it was his show, and he was excited–Sinatra sang "Chicago, Chicago" in his usual show business pizzazz style; Diana Ross did a performance with a whole orchestra that went on interminably, and then John, very simply, sang "Back Home Again" with just his guitar as an accompaniment. When the speakers' turn came–Rabin and Kissinger–they were both mulling over the emotions that had been evoked for them listening to John's song. I don't think either man was that familiar with John's music, but they were both touched enough by the lyrics to try to weave its sentiments into their remarks. I thought that said a lot about John's strength as a communicator. But it went right by Weintraub. At that point, he was basically climbing his own ladder.

At the time, Jerry's idol was Colonel Parker, Elvis Presley's manager, whose maxims he was given to quoting as if he were Moses on the mountain. After John superseded Elvis as RCA's number one recording artist, I suppose he even tried to *be* the colonel; although saying 'Colonel Weintraub' takes some getting used to. But the school of Colonel Parker had a very clear methodology: Get as much publicity as you can and if you don't have a story, make it up. With Jerry's rise to prominence in the entertainment industry, the stories pyramided, and so did the schemes that went with them. In exchange for his artists' services, Jerry was getting tithed, like a pope. First, he leveraged John's popularity to get major clients. Then he used the clients to get position. Then he let his position distract him from what he was doing for John, as well, I imagine, from what he was doing for others. Jackie Vernon's experience comes to mind. Having followed Jerry to Hollywood, hoping it would help him move along in his career, he fell on hard times. On some occasion in Hollywood, when Weintraub was waxing on about his generosity to strangers, I asked him if he would help set up something for Jackie. Let him open for one of his acts. He was in a position to help and he agreed. But it was only a gesture, and the follow-up fell between the cracks.

It was okay with me that Jerry was using his success with John to feather his own nest, just as long as it didn't impinge on John's career. In fact, after the success of "Rocky Mountain High," Jerry exacted a "private label" record company from RCA as part of the deal in getting John to sign with them again, and I ran it with him. I would have preferred instead had John moved then to a new recording company. RCA kept changing hands at the top and were always a year behind where John was in his work, always wanting the new records to be like the ones he had already done. Their judgment and their interests were increasingly misguided. But Weintraub wanted to stay with them because he could count on being in control.

The record company we started was called Windsong. John, Jerry, Milt and I were its principals. It came with benefits and enough in overhead to pay for offices and an apartment in New York, which I probably used more than anyone. Having a place to stay in Manhattan overnight inspired me to spend at least two days a week in the city popping into clubs, looking at new acts friends were recommending. I'd hang out at CBGBs, on the Bowery, disguised as an aging hipster. I immersed myself in the business, trying to find out what was happening. Not quite Clive Davis or Ahmet Ertegun, still I came to work ever hopeful. The third album we released on the Windsong label, in fact, was a monster hit. It was done by a group of John's friends, including Bill and Taffy Danoff, John's collaborators on 'Take Me Home, Country Roads,' who called themselves "The Starland Vocal Band." They were one of the best vocal groups I had heard in years. I had all sorts of ideas about promoting them.

But while I was the nominal president of the label, Jerry as res-

Fathers are less born to the manner than made from the ground up: two parts one's own experience of being fathered, two parts in blithe imitation of Father Knows Best, and six parts gleaned, if lucky, from the intuitions of one's better half. When issues about Michael or Amy surfaced as they were living through their respective childhoods, I confess to not always taking the time, or having the time, to think things through. I'd simply make the calls that were necessary at the time, and go on to the next thing.

ident sacker of cities had first dibs on the spoils if there were any. So when the band's single, 'Afternoon Delight,' soared to become a major hit, he took over its management, and immediately brought about its demise. Not that he did it intentionally. Rather he acted without giving it too much thought, if any, and put the band into a Saturday afternoon television series, a sitcom of sorts, whose only laughable quality was the show itself. They were four or five of the worst musical comedy shows that ever appeared on television–in my opinion. The band included four enormously talented people with a bent for comedy, but they couldn't overcome the bad writing and the bad production. This terrible show was in part responsible for the group not going anywhere; they were branded with their failure. I tried to work with them as a business manager because I saw them as essentially a great musical team. But for Jerry it was a peripheral act. Jerry's formula for handling things was simple. If it moved his game along he was for it.

He was a deal maker, rather than a builder. The old-time movie moguls were crude and tyrannical, but they built something; they were entrepreneurs. Jerry was more the carny guy, a gifted salesman. He'd send the private plane, there'd be girls, there'd be caviar and champagne, he'd tell you how much he loved you and loved what you did. And then he'd forget you.

In Hollywood, he had a big organization, but he delegated very little because he needed to control it all himself. He didn't like any-one second-guessing him. It even made him suspicious when you did your job. It deeply annoyed him the few times my name appeared in the trade press in connection with Windsong, usually in conjunction with Milt Okun or a new act. It would be no more than the perfunctory company announcement, but it was like brandishing a red flag in front of a bull.

Once, to rap my knuckles, he called me at night. I had developed a recording project in connection with a well-known cartoonist; someone in fact who used to spoof John in the papers. We were going to use one of his stock characters to create a recording and I had developed a promotion for it. Jerry called to tell me personally he wanted the project dropped: 'You have too much to do with this campaign. You're going to get too popular.' He was laughing as he uttered each sentence, but he was dead serious about it, and we never pursued the matter.

I finally got some satisfaction for my grievances one day in Los Angeles; it was like bearding the lion in his den. Our production company was putting together a John Denver Special for ABC, for which I was handling the finances. At the same time, John was putting the finishing touches on a new album and we were planning a concert tour. I'd flown in to be on hand for the final tying together of all three events. We were on the set of the television show and dozens of people were busy working and running around. At some point, I told the line producer that I wanted my name to appear on the scroll that comes up at the end of the show. I had worked on the show and I wanted a credit. It was Weintraub who had taught me to get the credit; the credit is more important than the money, he said.

The producer, astonished at my temerity or whatever, had run to Jerry to tell him what was going on and Jerry summoned me to his office. Everyone from the production staff was there. 'What's up, Hal?' Jerry liked nothing better than to toy with your feelings, even as he conceded the point. I told him what was up.

"Yeah, Hal. We decided that after the musicians, after everyone in the show is listed, we'll run your name. It'll be fun. Only we can't think of a title for you."

Could anything be sadder than to be told by "Man of the Year" that he couldn't solve the simplest of riddles? I shared my angry feelings about the matter and left Jerry to his own devices. Fifteen minutes later he called me back:

"Hal, we're going to put you down as executive consultant. It's an interesting title! You'll be in a good place. You'll have your own credit. " There was a long interlude of silence as I walked away and then the dynamos could be heard starting up again. The roar of the Hollywood workplace could be heard again. The momentary lapse in the proper order of things dissolved in the din. The kingdom was saved.

In 1977, Jerry moved John into the movie business and the movie, "Oh, God!," with George Burns, was an enormous success. At the time, it became the highest grossing comedy ever. John became a budding movie star. Weintraub, however, didn't follow up on it, at least not on behalf of his client. He kept coming up with vague ideas, but nothing was put together. I suspect that the studios, at that point, didn't want to work with John Denver because it meant Jerry had to be involved in an enormous way. Apparently I wasn't the only one who found him less than the ideal collaborator. Whatever the case, John never got to do another feature film under Jerry's management.

The loss to the entertainment industry of John's comic potential, not to get too carried away by the possibilities, was the environmen-

Geodesic dome in Louisiana created by Buckminster Fuller.

tal movement's gain. To help give weight and substance in this period to a general rethinking of environmental issues that was percolating up from the ground all over the place, John sank his teeth, and his money, into creating The Windstar Foundation. He had had an interest in doing this for a long time–long before it became fashionable to talk about caring for the environment–and to his credit he wasted no time, once he had the means, to put his clout behind his social conscience. There was an activist spirit in John that matched my own, even though I was more subdued about expressing it, and working with John in support of those interests was empowering. Not that John's example alone accounted for my interest. Dorothy too had been turning in that direction. After studying with the School of Inner Sense Development at Durham, N.C., she had become a psychic healer, working with private patients and lecturing in parapsychology, and her research in alternative methods of traditional medical treatments affected the thinking of everyone in our family. Windstar's founding was a converging of all our interests.

The initial board of directors was comprised of John, who was spiritual leader and our spokesman; Tom Crum, a teacher at a school for children in Aspen and a martial arts master whose specialty was conflict resolution, who had responsibility for developing the curriculum, and myself, who had charge of the organization and all financial matters.

The purpose of The Windstar Foundation, as we thought about it in those early years, was to develop an education research facility that would foster the concept of harmony: within ourselves, collectively, environmentally, globally. We meant it to be a place where people could develop ideas and concepts about living holistically as 'caretakers of the planet.' Indeed Windstar started to do good works even as it was inventing itself.

One of my first tasks was procuring a place to house Windstar and negotiating its purchase. The Trappist monastery in Snowmass was interested in selling its land and building and John and Tom had asked me to look into it. The asking price was $300,000 and I figured I would be masterful and negotiate a lower figure. But before I could mount my spiel, the head of the monastery, Father Michael Abdo, said to me, "Hal, we need $300,000 to move to a new place." Not that the Trappists wanted it, or that it was worth it, but that they needed it. Looking at one of the most spiritual men I have ever met, I understood anew the meaning of the word 'need,' and knew that 'need' was the only important aspect of the deal. Thus Windstar's business division entered the runup to the next millennium at the level of moral urgency rather than material worth, which was a demonstration project all by itself.

For that matter, it would have been cheaper to knock down the monastery and build another structure. It was a stone and metal construction that had become highly inefficient to heat. Instead we had the building redesigned and turned it into a demonstration project for passive and solar energy. Afterwards, Windstar became a principal supporter of Buckminster Fuller's work. Fuller built a geodesic dome on the property, with which Windstar began to experiment. Other projects included a full length film about the state of hunger in the world, which we made available to organizations and schools without charge, and which in turn led to John's appointment to President Carter's Commission on World Hunger, for which he went to Washington regularly with full agenda. Windstar also did a number of films on environmental concerns, and through a series of position papers helped support passage of the Alaska Wildlife bill.

Through the first 10 years of Windstar's existence, at least 70 percent of its costs came from John's own pocket, which was a lot more generous than he needed to be. And of course that generosity was my domain to rationalize. If for no one else, I had to rationalize it to myself. I had to rethink the uses of money and the meaning of philanthropy. After John's great success in the Seventies, there wasn't a day that went by that his mail didn't have a couple of dozen requests for help from one cause or another. His tendency was to want to be the great benefactor.

Once, out of concern for Bucky Fuller's dwindling financial circumstances, John dispatched me to his office in Philadelphia, where I spent a day with Bucky's staff to see if I could bring order to the great man's financial affairs. At lunch, Bucky regaled me with stories of his boyhood and I shared some of mine. I can't say I compre-hended everything he tried to explain, or that he got all of what I told him about where I was coming from. But one thing came through clearly—at the level of those boyhoods, we were traveling in the same direction, flags flying, arms outstretched. Only I was doing it more prudently.

Meanwhile, despite the annoyance of Weintraub's intensifying self-promotion, and its effect on my gastric juices, it continued to be an over-the-top time working with John. His music had made him a 'superstar' and I found it an interesting phenomenon to be around, both for the sheer nuttiness of it, and for the shared enjoyment it provided. We'd leave a concert and there'd be hundreds of people outside the arena waiting to get a glimpse of John—watching the show as "the show" continued. We'd leave in a three-car caravan and sometimes I'd serve as the smoke screen, riding in the limo, so that John could go in one of the other cars and avoid the crush. One night, someone came up to me and offered $500 for John's coffee cup. Was this reverence or dementia? Five hundred? For $500, I said, I'll give you two cups, and a pound of coffee.

Breathing In, Breathing Out

On the day of the much anticipated reunion with the "New York Indians," I woke like a boy about to go off on a favorite trip. I pushed all malign thoughts out of my head. On my morning constitutional, I walked for miles, until I was sweating like a pig. I tried to grasp the

notion of 'time passing,' thinking about 'olden times.' Was 25 years a lot of time or a little bit of time? I suppose it depended on who was doing the measuring. Thomas Wolfe once said you can't go home again, but it is inevitable to want to try. It wasn't to see the old buildings that I yearned, I told myself, but rather to feel again the sense of a place where I was a member in a shared life. So many things that I once thought imperishable had disappeared from the Bronx. Jennings Street market had been dismantled. The Minford Place Synagogue had been demolished. Charlotte Street had been leveled. There had been not only a sea change in the local population, but a deep-sea change. That feeling of belonging seemed to mean something all on its own. Could it be conjured up one more time simply by coming together? It was an early fall, and the woods around Weston, our home in Connecticut, were already tinged with autumnal colors. Were we being autumnal within ourselves? Who would I see? Would they remember me? Would I be recognized? Would I recognize them?

The place itself where we met was where several roads converged onto a traffic circle and then pinwheeled off again in different directions. The symbolism seemed apt. We had come together like that as children, traveling for awhile in the same circular course, and then going off in different directions when we joined the adult world. What we had come together again to explore was that circle—not the comfortable physical zone we shared, but a spiritual space that was like the eye of a storm.

Driving down from Connecticut, I recalled the vertigo I felt early one evening when one of my old friends paid an unexpected call at my office. Steve and I were meeting in the conference room with a couple of bankers, trying to arrange financing for one of our clients. There were six of us around the table, and I was leading the discussion, driving home a point. Our secretary had left for the day and we were ensconced in a setting that I thought of as 'boardroom conditions.'

Suddenly the door to the front office opened and in walked Max. Not Max Roach, or Maxwell Cohen; but Max Klein. Bush jacket, dungarees, short and plump. He looked a little bit, as he appeared there, like Harpo Marx: the impish leer, the head of golden curls, the eyebrows raised in wonder. He was fresh from the day shift at the Morgan post office. For an instant, he took us in with the same show of curiosity that the rest of us had for him. I could feel everyone at the table drawing back as if they were seeing a creature from Mars. Then before I could stop him, Max caught me in his gaze, his face lighting up, and said: 'Peewee!! How are you doing?' Nobody knew what to make of this. Nor frankly did I. Though I'm short, I'm tall by comparison with Max. What could I say in explanation? Collecting myself, I quickly rose to my feet, put an arm around my old friend, walked him to the front office, tweaked both cheeks, let him tweak mine, and said I'd see him later. Then I went back to the table full of bankers and finished what I was saying. Later I laughed about the incident, but at the same time the surprise of it took me down a notch, like a sudden drop of altitude, before I recovered. How would I manage it when everyone got together? Dorothy approached the whole thing with the aplomb that comes with being a mother of two. It was going to be the first time she'd seen me in the context of a huge family.

Then there they were, all the faces I knew, as if time had stood still. One or two faces were hiding behind beards, but their voices gave them away. I thought I might not remember names, but the names came unbidden. It was amazing how soulful it felt just to say them. The passage of time had made what was once ordinary holiness itself. At the same time, it came to me how little we knew about each other. Despite the fact that we had lived in such intimate regard, there was so much taken for granted. Some guys knew me only by a nickname and still held on to that. One guy came with his parents, and some with sisters who wanted to see us, too–to see us all together. They too had come with a sense that by being there, all in the same place again, we might recover the feeling of membership.

And true enough, the small hall rented for the occasion swelled with talk–the talk of olden times–and lifted us into another realm. For one last time–or so I thought, we drove into the circle and went round and round. All was well in that kingdom. That night, my dreams went all over the place. In the morning I woke with the pressing thought that I needed to go on a journey, but not the kind of journey a ticket agent could help me with. The thought was still puzzling me when, a couple of weeks later, a most amazing coincidence took place. Something 'far out,' as John would say.

8

Theater, Darling?

I loved going to California. I loved the pink patina of the Beverly Hills Hotel. It is the hotel where all the movie moguls and would-be movie moguls gather in the morning to get the fires-in-their-bellies stocked for the day ahead. For the price of a lanai, you could hold poolside meetings; you could pretend to be a sheik at a desert oasis. It would have been easy to move out there. My heart just wasn't in it. People in the business need to hold on to your arm when they talk to you. I didn't want to spend the kind of time there that would have been needed to make the thing work.

Besides it would have been suicide trying to deal with Weintraub on a daily basis. By 1980, he was carrying on like a tailored god. He wanted more of this pie, more of that pie. His appetite had become insatiable. If you did something as simple as stand your ground with him, he'd treat you as the class enemy.

One time–and this was a burlesque of the low-level warfare we were engaged in–I had just come into L.A. to catch the last stop on a John Denver concert tour. I had checked into the Beverly Hills hotel and gone through my usual routine of stress reduction, which consisted essentially of a game of tennis with the house pro. Hoping to savor a quiet hour before I had to meet with Weintraub, I went down to the lounge for breakfast.

I was all alone, reading *The New York Times*. And in he walked with his entourage. He had a meeting elsewhere in the room, but he spotted me, and in a second he and his men encircled my table. It was like being caught at the Jennings Street market by kids from

West Farms Road: Weintraub, Finkelstein (Jerry's lawyer), Bonafede (Sal was Jerry's right-hand man, and actually my friend), and a couple of other sycophants. In his most sincere voice, alluding to the agenda of our meeting an hour away, Jerry said: "I'm the toughest

Renewing our marriage vows in 1983.

guy you're ever going to meet in your life." In that context, the toughest guy I could think of was Frankenstein. And Sal said, "Yeah, Hal. Listen to him! He's the toughest guy you'll ever meet." Comedy or tragedy? My eggs were getting cold! My breakfast was ruined!

Another time Jerry telephoned me at a spa. I'd left a message for Jerry to call me, but it was a mistake to answer the call; I was much too relaxed to deal with a sacker of cities. I had been trying to negotiate a raise in salary for John's brother, Ron, who worked for us at Windsong Records, and when I made my pitch, Jerry laced into me. I might as well have been trying to take money out of his pocket. He said he had a dossier on me. He let me know all the bad things he thought I had done. He went berserk with self-righteousness. I could feel a week-long effort of psychic rebuilding leeching out through my pores. My blood pressure rose giddily. I hung up the phone and seethed. A few minutes ticked away and once more I was paged to the phone: Weintraub again.

"Hal, we shouldn't fight! The guy isn't worth it! We have a long relationship! I want to make up! I love you!"

Such love no man should have to endure.

Much as I was itching to expand my repertoire, do new things, use my experience in new-found ways, I could see L.A. at that point

Dorothy and John.

wasn't going to be for me. If Weintraub was a candidate for the King of Hollywood, that was a kingdom I would give short shrift to. In fact, other siren voices were already beckoning.

Actually it was less the voices than a particular smile. I'd just boarded a flight at Kennedy on my way to California. I was making my way toward the back, and there, bigger than life smiling up at me from his seat, was one of the New York Indians who, I suddenly realized, hadn't been to our Bronx reunion a few months earlier. No one had thought to contact him.

He, with his family, had moved from the Bronx in that first wave out to the suburbs after the war, and had dropped out of our orbit. They had gone only to Queens, 10 miles away as the crow flies, but it might as well have been to another continent. *"Il est disparu,"* we would say on the corner of Boston Road and E. 173rd Street when anyone wondered about Larry Crane. Larry had disappeared from our mental screens, and we from his. It had been 40 years since we'd seen one another, but in outward appearances we hadn't changed all that much. We recognized each other instantly.

He had the same shock of red hair as when I'd last seen him, the same cluster of freckles across the bridge of his nose, and especially the same Howdy Doody smile that no one could match for toothy amiability. To me, he always seemed somewhat better cared for than the rest of us, and I'd always attributed it to his having two parents who were native-born Americans. Compared to him, we seemed to be neglected kids, even if we were happy to be neglected.

We found seats together and lost ourselves in reminiscences. He was charming, and flattered my conceits. At some point, he asked if I knew anything about the theater. He was involved in a theatrical venture. He was trying to do a musical. There were no stars. Everyone involved was doing it for scale. It was about the first man and the first woman, Harry and Mary, It was called "Earthlings." Was I interested?

There was no full script yet. But being a novice in that particular aspect of the business–and eager to learn about it–I didn't see how not having a script to begin with would be a problem. He seemed to have a good sense of what the story was about. If I was interested, why didn't we meet when I got back to New York, Larry suggested. He'd have the composer, Earl Wilson, Jr. play me the score and Otto Maximillian, who was the director and choreographer, describe the scenario.

Wilson had already written the songs for a successful long-running show. I was curious. What I liked particularly about the project was that it was family fare. There didn't seem to be anything like it around. The music sounded very good. I did my arithmetic again; I talked to Crane. I may have even wavered a bit, as is my wont. In the end though, I agreed to come into the show as a co-producer.

We blocked out what we needed to do and started in July, hoping to open off-Broadway in September. The theater we were going to open in wasn't exactly a legitimate playhouse–in another incarnation it had been Lou Walters' Latin Quarter, a Broadway night club that I was always reading about in the tabloids when I was kid–but it suited my fantasies. Broadway and what it stood for theatrically was Mecca for me, not Hollywood. When we Indians discovered Shubert's Alley, we figured out that if we waited until after the curtains had gone up and gave the guy at the door a few bucks, they'd let us stand in back of the orchestra, just so long as we didn't make ourselves conspicuous, which was hard not to do because we hadn't yet mastered the rules of civility. But the theater we managed to see that way–missing the opening moments–registered with my sensibilities. The images still shine in my memory. The movies were great, but theater somehow meant more. And once bitten, forever smitten.

Being a producer is a matter of solving paradoxes, one after the other, until either none is left, or what's left does you in. In our case, the first paradox had to do with a place to work, and proved to be the only one we could solve. To get a place in which to put the show together, we needed money, and in order to get the money we needed a place. Crane found the Playboy Club Resort in Great Gorge, New Jersey, willing to give the cast room and board in exchange for eight performances a week.

It was out-of-town, but not that far that we couldn't take liberties in our promotion: "Why not see a Broadway show while you're enjoying lunch," one flyer read. "Or on Monday nights for drinks." I think we charged $5 at the door to anyone who came in off the street, and nothing to the Club's guests.

A couple of times a week, we'd run potential backers out to see the show. If it was a long weekend, I'd take a room at the inn. I was just starting to run to keep in shape, and I'd run a couple of miles with one of the investors, who would come down from Boston to see how things were going.

My fantasy was that rehearsals were going to be like the ones I'd seen in the Mickey Rooney-Judy Garland movies when I was a kid: 'We're putting on a play,' they used to say; 'we'll work from nine to five; we'll make it better. I've got the chicken! You've got the hen! Let's dance!'

But on the first day of rehearsals at the Playboy Club, the union representative came down and everybody had to sign union cards. Suddenly union rules were being quoted. There was talk of grievances. Quick as a flash, I became big business, trying to exploit labor. I was the heavy, and there's Paul Muni and John Garfield, the downtrodden guys, on the other side.

Then some of the cast demanded that they be treated as stars, even though we had talked about giving everyone equal billing. I met with Equity and worked things out, but some of the cast insisted they'd be working under duress. Finally, even putting the invest-

With Earl Wilson and his wife at a performance of Earthlings.

ment together became difficult to do. Our biggest angel was a Sugar Daddy who wanted his leggy mistress to be in the chorus, which worked out well, especially for him. But other angels were harder to convince. Occasionally, Larry and I took turns doubling as maitre-d's, just so that we could seat prospective investors at the tables with the appropriate sight lines. In Crane's zeal, he would sometimes get into hassles about who got to sit where.

As if what we were dealing with wasn't complicated enough, late in August the owner of the theater we had reserved informed us that he was broke. He didn't have the money to pay his rent promptly. We'd given him $10,000 as a deposit for the dates we were projecting. Now, unless we came up with another five, he was saying, it was unlikely we'd be able to open the show there. What do you do in a case like that? You've got $10 grand there! Is there any place to go? No, of course not! You have to try to help the guy.

But the ultimate paradox was a show without a book, or one that worked, and we couldn't solve that one. That paradox cleaved us in two, and no one seemed to notice. Everybody was so in love with what they were doing, they couldn't see the forest for the trees. To a degree, I sympathized. The songs were full of wonderful metaphors about the human condition. The Earthlings had gone from their Edenic beginnings to a crazy frenetic society, and the first man turned into someone who could kill other earthlings: Let's wake up from this bad dream! Like everybody else, I identified with the spiritual qualities of the story. But unless a song was being sung, nothing was happening on the stage. Without a story, it wasn't musical theater.

With each passing day, my angst grew, and a universe opened up between my idea of what we were doing and my partner's. What I wanted from the show, along with the fun of doing it, was success and profit for all the backers. What my partner was looking for seemed to be psychic redemption. I'd leave him alone in the theater for a minute and he'd have everyone in the company doing meditation. "What are you doing," I'd say apoplectically, "we're running out of time! The clock is ticking! We're tightly budgeted! We're spending money! We're supposed to be working! This isn't Paradise yet!" He'd smile back, blissed out. He was an early earthling.

In the hope of salvaging something, I tried to stage a palace upheaval and take control of the production, but to no avail. The production just wasn't good enough yet to sustain a Broadway audience. I could do nothing to offset the lack of a good book. We had just enough money to squeeze by to the projected opening. But we'd be hopelessly in hock before the first week was out. So two weeks before we were supposed to open, I sat everyone down, had a final meeting, and closed the show.

The whole thing was demoralizing. It is hard to let go, even when it is the rational thing to do. In fact, we continued to try to figure out ways to make it work after it closed. Wilson and Maximillian restaged it in workshop form and I put more money into it. Still nothing came of it.

But I was hooked on producing theater. The forms of work involved appealed to my obsessions, especially those moments when collectively we brought an intense focus to bear on what we were doing. That's always been my forte, whether in love or war; whether it had to do with deals or my children. I saw that to make artistic decisions, I didn't have to carry myself as an artist. I just had to put myself into the struggle. It is axiomatic in the theater that up until opening night, it is an artistic struggle. But then the play turns into a business. I figured I could grow into the part very nicely.

My dilemma, at first, was that if I pursued the theater, I'd have to give up running the business I had with Steve. When it came down to it, I felt I couldn't do both. I took the better part of a year to sort it out in my mind. It was as if I was contemplating the end of a long marriage, which in a way it was. In the end, Steve helped me to do it by empathizing with what I wanted, even though it made little sense to him. Few spouses could have been as reasonable in contemplating divorce. He was more understanding about it than a lot of our clients. Judith Light's protest that I needed to be with her, on stage, when she would hold high her Oscar, was the kindest one of all. But I was as adamant about it as I was touched. The one client I took with me was John Denver, which at that point was like taking my brother along, or rather going along with him. His standing in the recording industry was taking a hit, but his career was still going strong, and my work for him kept the bills paid.

In Aspen, where we'd begun to spend more and more of our family life, I formed a small investment company with Robert

Courson, a California real estate developer, whom I spotted as someone who shared my sense of entrepreneurial adventure when we first met. We called it The Aspen Company, which we still operate. We had a mutual interest in the theater, as well as in other pursuits, and became close friends. Initially we each invested $5,000 to capitalize

With Bobby Courson (far right) I formed the Aspen Co.

our company, and agreed to cultivate only interests of a visceral nature. If we couldn't dance to it, we didn't want to be in it. Our first investment, in fact, was to purchase units in various Hard Rock Cafes. We also thought about buying an interest in a limousine service, so that we could use the cars to see our restaurants and theatrical projects, but then we dropped that idea as being too frivolous, even for members of the "Aspen Club." Our approach wasn't exactly Harvard Business School, but it worked for us. It was a game, but a game I wanted to demonstrate prowess in.

The theater producing community in New York isn't that big, but it's fairly democratic as these things go. If there is a place at the table and you take it, you get dealt a hand. The paint on the walls of the office I'd found on Times Square had hardly dried when Wayne Adams called with a project. We'd met when I was doing Earthlings and stayed in touch. He wanted me to fly with him to Chicago to see a new production of a Sam Shepard play called "True West," which

165

he thought we might do in New York. As much as the play, he also wanted me to see the acting company doing it: a group of young iconoclasts who called themselves Steppenwolf. Joseph Papp had done "True West" in New York a couple of seasons earlier and Shepard, along with the critics, had roundly condemned his production of it. Steppenwolf's director Gary Sinise had given the play a different reading.

I knew nothing about any of this, neither about Shepard's work, nor Steppenwolf's, except for what Wayne could relate between the departing and arriving gates. If I had simply read the play beforehand, I probably would have passed on it. The script, as written, was too full of obscure allusions for me. Fortunately there was no time; there was just a moment to decide whether or not I'd go to Chicago and I said yes. It was a case where ignorance is bliss.

That night in Chicago, on Steppenwolf's proscenium, was a revelation for me. Shepard's words came off the page powerfully transformed and I was introduced to the acting of John Malkovich. I'd never seen an actor so wedded to his part. His performance was all edge: brooding, malevolent, mercurial. It was a retelling of Cain and Abel; an encounter between two brothers caught in an undertow of psychic violence that some families seem born to. And it was pure theater. I left there feeling not that I wanted to do this play, but compelled to do it.

Over the next few months, I returned to see the play several times and came to know a great many of the players in the Steppenwolf Company. The visits were by way of pilgrimages. One time I brought a potential angel, who didn't get the play at all, and stumbled from the theater baffled by my enthusiasm.

But, in fact, the financial backing was the easiest thing to come by in this project. The hard sell was the Steppenwolf Company itself, many of whom felt that if "True West" would succeed in New York, those who would succeed with it–Malkovich and Sinise–would leave Steppenwolf and Steppenwolf would come apart. Malkovich himself wasn't sure what he wanted to do. He wanted to go and he didn't.

He worried about Steppenwolf and didn't. In the end, it all fell into place. I didn't have to pull any rabbits out of a hat.

We moved the Steppenwolf crew into apartments in midtown. We brought the Cherry Lane Theater in Greenwich Village out of mothballs and refurbished it. Most importantly, we talked Sinise who had come to New York to direct the play into acting in it as well, opposite Malkovich, which meant vintage Steppenwolf. We filled both barrels–and if you drink too much of that *cru*, they say, it gets in your blood.

We had a few days of rehearsal and five previews, and then we opened. The critics loved the production. Stanley Crouch, in the *Village Voice*, called it "American perfection." The other reviews expounded from there. The reviews were so generally ecstatic that people said I wrote them myself. But then we had to parlay the acclaim into getting people to the theater; into getting them from uptown downtown, which took some guile and not a little perseverance

I had kids sniping posters on boardings and people giving out flyers; we used every campaign we could. We had made a conscious decision not to ballyhoo the show and let New York 'discover' it. We worked at it, and worked at it. In fact, it took six to eight months to develop a momentum. Even though we had the reviews, we weren't selling out: the demand had to be built up.

And then the buzz went out on it. Eventually we did a film of the play for television, which Public Television aired. We filmed the week we made our first cast change, and because of scheduling problems it didn't get televised until six months later. But I think what happened was that in the interim period someone got hold of a copy of the television tape and circulated it throughout the Hollywood community. Word of mouth did the rest, for the show and for Malkovich, the actor, alike. We had become a hot ticket. (The other hot sell that year was Harvey Fierstein's "Torch Song Trilogy," which was playing uptown.) Every Hollywood personality, director, producer, and actor who came to town called about seats. It became an all-consuming and exciting job keeping up with the momentum of the play.

Periodically I'd come down to the Cherry Lane Theater for meetings with advertising people, etc. and afterwards sit on the stairs in the wings, looking through the banister at particular scenes I enjoyed. I'd be hard-pressed to say whether I was feeling man or boy then. I certainly was as mesmerized as I was when I was a boy watching actors on the stage. I could tell by the sound of the laughter that punctuated the speeches, and floated back to where we were meeting, where they were in the play. If I timed it right, I'd come in on cue to watch a scene I liked.

It would be years before I could see what I'd actually accomplished in keeping up my end of what we were doing together. Had I realized how much of a success we had, I probably would have brought it uptown, and Malkovich and Sinise probably would have stayed another six months. Malkovich probably would have won a Tony award. It would have cost half a million to transfer the show, but we had a band of angels who were true blue, and would have come along. I just lacked the confidence to go for it. I was so enmeshed in the production and in keeping it going that I was short-sighted. On the other hand, I'm also not one to change winners in midstream; we were doing well where we were. Everyone got out of the experience just about what they wanted.

The only thing I didn't get and that I would have wanted was to have John Denver move into Sinise's role. For him the play's emotional charge was as close to the bone as you can get. He had seen a preview of the play the night before it opened and was deeply affected by it, along with everyone else. I thought it would be a great learning experience for him to act on stage with Malkovich: they had a nice affinity. I had introduced them to each other and, as I hoped, they liked one another, two boys from the midwest, who respected each other's talent. In fact, I was always trying to weave John into my plots. I had the fantasy that if "Earthlings" had turned out to be more substantial than it was and a film was made of it, I'd cast John as Harry, the first man. With hindsight, I can see that in 1983 John had needed to make a transition from where he was professionally and personally.

In any case, the black ink defined me, for that moment at least, as one of the theater's leading producing lights, be it ever so humble. With production costs as they were in the industry, it had become the exception rather than the rule to see a straight dramatic theatrical production make money. Black ink was comparable to a

Broadway before WWI.

platinum record. Even in the provinces, the credit of a successful show worked magic. The bankers who Bobby Courson dealt with in his real estate investments were so impressed with his having helped to make so complex a work so successful an enterprise that they put extra stars next to his credit rating.

I also started to become a student of the theater and took as a mentor one of my Connecticut Yankee neighbors, Alan Lewis, who was a Shakespearean expert, a theatrical writer, and a theater critic for the local *Bridgeport Post*. He had developed Parkinson's disease and was finding it difficult to get around, so we struck a deal. In exchange for my driving him into Manhattan to openings, he'd take me along as his guest. And on the one-and-a-half hour ride back home, we'd dissect what we had seen. For me, it was an experience of high order, a kind of vetting. I always came away from those encounters with a surer sense of intellectual polish. Just as you don't have to be a practicing artist to be artistic, you don't have to be a practicing intellectual to express your intellect; the theater is its own realm. It was a humbling discovery.

Not that the cockiness I felt about my business acumen softened, or that I suddenly found purpose, as I wondered about it as a kid. It was more a residual humanism–Bronx melodies–coming back into the story in another register. After all, Broadway isn't that far from the Bronx, and in the Bronx I was taught that left to my own devices I'd be a fool not to try to make my mark in a meaningful way. Step up to the plate, darling, and hit the ball!

Over the next couple of years, what I earned in the theater I might have spent, more or less, on lunches at the Carnegie deli: it wasn't much. But what I learned was more than I could pay for. For one thing, I learned how philosophically to defend myself against the blows when things didn't work out. Didn't the philosophers say that, at 50, the mature mind emerges? In fact, no sooner had "True West" established itself as hale and hearty than another budding maestro, Mace Newfeld, asked my help in saving a doomed project, and I jumped into the fray again, anticipating that I'd see myself celebrated as the *wunderkind* of 1983.

Mace had brought a revue, starring "The Flying Karamazov Brothers," into the newly refurbished Ritz Theater on Broadway and found, as I had with "True West," that despite very good notices, it wasn't stirring up an audience. I thought I could help by replicating what I had just done. It didn't work that way though. The economics of downtown didn't travel uptown so well, or at least it had to be reconfigured. Before we figured it out, we had simply run out of time and had to close the show. Doing this kind of work is akin to erecting a scaffolding around a moving object that's crossing a rope bridge, before the fraying strands of rope give way. You don't have room or time for too many miscalculations or rest stops along the way.

London was another story, as reasonable a place to do business in the theater, at that point, as New York was becoming unreasonable; as thick in theater culture as L.A. was thin. Not only a thick theater culture, but different. A place where it was never considered frivolous to ask, 'Theatre, darling?' I was brought into it by two veteran theatrical producers, Frank Gero and Fred Zollo, who worked together on projects in New York. They were for me the personification of professional camaraderie in the business. If they had a project, they showed it around. There was always room for an extra partner, or relationship. Everybody always had need for some kind of help. None of us had enough money or contacts to do everything on our own. The two of them had been conducting their own trans-Atlantic seminar on how the vivacity of London's theatrical life, given the common language, might be made to work for Broadway, or at least Broadway producers like ourselves. Joseph Papp had the same ideas for the Public Theater. My interests converged with theirs and I joined the seminar. When the English pound dropped to nearly par with the dollar—the fall of 1984—the seminar heated up. When Gero brought in Stephen Poliakoff's 'Breaking the Silence' to read, along with the reviews, the seminar swung into action, which we mobilized into a New York-limited partnership.

Actually, all we had to do was set up the financial instruments that allowed us to carry on a legal business in London: the creative end of it was already in place, including the actors (Royal Shakespeare Company), the director (Ron Daniels), and the theater (The Mermaid). Poliakoff had written the story of an aristocratic Russian family, living in a railroad boxcar amidst the Russian revolution, while the paterfamilias Nikolai is working to put the finishing touches on his invention of talking pictures. It was by turns brilliant comedy and a brilliant thriller. The title, 'Breaking the Silence,' referred to how the Revolution, in its delayed effect on this family, liberated Nikolai's wife and family servant, even while the son, and heir apparent, was turning into a spineless conformist. My mother particularly would have enjoyed the ironies.

No sooner did we get that play running on the West End than we

Theater on Leicester Square, London.

were doing another, a reworking of 'Camille,' by Pam Gems, which had been done initially by the RSC. And then another: David Mamet's 'Glengarry Glen Ross,' which the National Theater had done, and which had already played in New York. Before a year was out, I had added to that trio of productions with a fourth that I did on my own, a new play by an American writer, Wesley Moore, called 'Swim Visit.'

By then, I was passing through Heathrow, coming and going, so regularly that the customs agents were beginning to show me the interest reserved for drug couriers. Maybe they still saw me as a herald from the Sixties: the bright cast of my brown eyes, the slightly manic facial expressions. Besides working to build up Woodrun Management, I was still handling Denver's business affairs fulltime and managed all of these involvements only by keeping on the go. But all I was carrying in my bags, besides their country's native genius in manuscript form, were extra socks and underwear that Dorothy made sure I took along.

The appeal for me of doing Moore's play was the sheer fact of being able to do a full-scale production in London for what a showcase production cost in New York. I figured I would take a month off and immerse myself in what needed to be done. What better way to learn what the questions are? But if you think it was romantic, forget it. London was, for me, still a strange city. I recognized tourist attractions when I saw them in passing, but the workaday life had to be put together from scratch, and worked at. A theater (the Donmar Warehouse) had to be rented; Actors Equity had to be made happy because I was bringing over an American actress for the lead; a dozen collegial relationships had to be assembled, integrated, and consulted; and I had to do the practical things. Some afternoons I'd stand in Covent Garden doing anything I could think of to shill an audience for 'Swim Visit.' Interesting? Yes. Difficult? More difficult than anything I had done.

When I first came to London as part of Denver's retinue, I stayed at the Inn on the Park, a very chic place. As a producer, I worked my way down the chain to a nicely discreet hotel on the Four Dials Road, a few blocks from Covent Garden; it was a hotel full of travelers, and I was one among them. So even though I was in London, the English were mostly only in the background. The theater was nearby and I could walk everywhere. There was no chance of my getting lost in the tube. But dinner proved daunting. I got ptomaine poisoning immediately, or else it was just the Roumanian flu. After that, I didn't know what to eat, except maybe a potato on the run.

One moonless night, I ran into Harvey Fierstein at the Potato Shop in Covent Garden. He was in London doing 'Torch Song Trilogy' and standing in back of me in the queue. I was the last person he expected to see that night in that potato shop. I was supposed to be in Connecticut doing his taxes. In his deeply resonant voice, he said, 'Hal, what are you doing here?' I said: 'What are you doing here?' He said, 'I'm eating potatoes, Hal!' And then, clutching our potatoes, we ran out into the cold, blustery miserable streets pretending: he to be a queen of the theater, and I a prince.

9

Perhaps Love

After my stay in London, I would dream about it obsessively. First acts, strictly first acts. I'd wake from the dream vaguely uncertain about where I was, here or there. My mind was still caught up in trying to block the scene. And often I'd be wakened from these dream states by John, calling from half-way around the world, checking in with me in between stops on a tour.

In one memorable dream sequence, Bobby Mendelson and I

appear on stage together. I am trying to explain to him how he needs to move from one place on the stage to another. The next minute we are walking along Jennings Street, chalking the words, V for victory! on the sides of buildings; I am an 11-year-old again. I can hear myself addressing my parents about the need for 'sound' thinking. I am amplifying myself in the American idiom and I am feeling good. I am feeling as if I've just beaten Hitler's army myself.

But before the dream could get any zanier, I'd realize that the bell that had been ringing in the background was my phone and wake up: John was calling from Leningrad. I had to struggle for a few seconds to understand what John was doing in Leningrad, and then it came back to me.

The world was going through some complicated structural changes that summer after London: South Africa, Poland, Central America; all kinds of insurgencies; and *perestroika*. John was giving a series of concerts, from Leningrad to Moscow, serving unofficially as a troubadour of goodwill. He was calling with a report about the state of Soviet show business. We were interested in learning more about it and working with it. He was also filling me in on his schedule, so that we could coordinate a trip to China. Aside from everything else that was happening–or maybe because of it–we were going global. My classmates at the Bernard Baruch School of Business at City College would have been proud of me; Baruch himself would have been delighted.

In China, I got to deliver a treatise on free market venture capitalism. We wanted to do a John Denver worldwide TV special via satellite from Beijing, and took over a production and technical team of advisors to sell the Chinese government on the idea. We wanted them to be partners with us in a global television joint venture, a first of its kind for China. The name of George Bush may not yet have meant anything to the average Chinese at that point, but John Denver's name and music were household items. Years before, in fact, when Chou-en-lai, then Premier of China, had come to New York to address the United Nations and the Mayor had offered to entertain the Premier, the Mayor's office fielded a call from the Chinese delegation, asking for John Denver to appear. John happened to be in town, performed as requested, and made friends. Now we hoped to help the Chinese to learn a new technology.

We met with the Chinese network–CCTV, which was their version of ABC, NBC and CBS all rolled up into one inscrutable bureaucracy. They wanted to do the show, but they didn't understand capitalism or how it works in the modern marketplace; nor did the delegation who came to see us seem to care one way or another. They were interested mostly, I think, in their perks.

They loved to come to the Great Wall Hotel in Beijing for the luncheons we catered for them. And one night, we 'honored' them with a 12-course banquet. Everyone in their group was angling for a trip to the U.S. But the concept of 'fifty-fifty' they didn't understand. They understood, but they didn't want. They loved John, but when it came to a business deal, they preferred the picture they had in their heads rather than the one I drew for them.

John wasn't going to charge for his services and we weren't going to charge for the technical equipment that we would leave behind. We would pay everyone else who worked on the show. If the

We wanted to do a John Denver worldwide TV special via satellite from Beijing, and brought over a production and technical team of advisors to sell the Chinese government on the idea. I got to deliver a treatise on free market venture capitalism.

show made money, we'd split it with the Chinese government.

They took us around to look at possible sites and we negotiated. We thought at first we would do the show from the Great Wall, but once we saw it, it seemed too impractical. Beyond its enormity, what more was there? How about the Forbidden Palace, we asked. We could set up a stage in one of the courtyards, bring in a crowd of people and film from a helicopter. They went berserk at the thought.

'How many people were we talking about?'

'Three thousand, five thousand?'

They went crazy. Three thousand people together in one spot? It could turn into a mini-revolution!

'How about Tianamen Square then'?

Every place we named presented a problem. They were willing to give us their cooperation–but for one million dollars–what we called below-the-line expenses. For a million, they would help us through the bureaucracy and provide us with what they called internal transportation, i.e. help us get from city to city with all our paraphernalia. Apparently, they had already done business with a production company of an L.A.-based sitcom, which obviously left behind a vaunted notion of what the American market could bring. I tried being philosophical about the difficulties.

In the mornings, before we'd meet, suited in shorts and a Walkman plugged into my ears, I ran miles through Beijing's streets, which swarmed with bikers and pedestrians and absolutely invited one's participation. Everything imaginable was being hauled and carried along in a great display of leg power. If here I was no longer of the people, I could at least be among them, running. After one such run, carried forward by the spiritual lift of doing it, I gave a rousing 40-minute dissertation to the CCTV bureaucrats on the nature of partnerships, winding up with an equally rousing explanation of why it was for them a no-lose situation. For added measure, I threw in a dissertation on the television world, another on the entertainment business, and one about double-entry bookkeeping, which they particularly enjoyed hearing, although maybe not in the way I intended. Bill Davis, an Emmy award-winning director, who we invited to work with us, was brought to his feet by my performance. For him, I had delivered the Olivier of my career. Not so to our Chinese counterparts.

Afterwards they showed a willingness to compromise on their price, but only with great parsimony, and they had started from such lofty expectations. We wanted to do a good thing, but not an impractical thing. Where it came to being practical, I was School of Baruch. In the midst of the discussions, I had a vision of Kahn and Shore, fluttering above the proceedings like my angels, reminding me that being on the job meant I was in charge. Alas and alack, in the case of China, this was not to be. A thousand flowers had been planted and none had bloomed.

But while the satellite-transmission-from-Beijing deal was never consummated, the experience of having visited a 'real star' of the planet–the state's political repressiveness notwithstanding–had a salutary effect on my mentality. Your eye grows its own consciousness. You learn love of country; in the same way, you learn love of planet.

Actually what made traveling with John so much fun and so interesting often was this deep respect for the real 'stars' on the planet. His eye for them was well-developed; I think he lived to see the next 'new' place. And he liked to teach, one on one, what he was learning in his seeing. Homespun he might sound, like a latter-day Will Rogers, but his planetary consciousness was as sophisticated as the best of our scientists. I'll always remember him in Beijing, arriving from Moscow, two places where he was known to people of every rank, and warmly welcomed. He was full of good feeling.

It was the last night of our talks there and he gave an impromptu concert for the American community: just he with his guitar, singing about the longings of the heart, the dream of freedom, and the pleasures of home-grown tomatoes, three of his themes. He was at his best in these moments, beyond the business of it, which he happily left to me. If we departed from China empty-handed, we left behind lots of goodwill.

John on the phone from Leningrad; John on the phone from Hanoi. He had moved into a new phase of his career, and was trying to get grounded again after a hard couple of years in his personal life. In 1981, his father, Dutch, whom he admired as much if not more than anyone else in this world, had died suddenly. A year later his marriage to Annie had ended, despite all their efforts to put things right. Then, in the spring of 1984, out of the blue, he broke with Weintraub.

Actually the break with Weintraub didn't exactly come out of the blue, but it did seem abrupt. I remember Jerry's aggrieved call, blind with rage, after he'd had the argument with John that would keep them from talking to one another for 10 years:

"John and I are quits!! I've got a contract with him and he is going to pay!! I'm going to get Louis Nizer and get every penny due me!! It's going to cost that son of ....' or words to that effect. He bel-

Denver in Moscow.

lowed as only wounded pride can. Nothing I could say would stem his tirade. Their meeting that morning, trying to resolve a long relationship that was going awry, kicked up so much heat that blows were avoided only on the physical level. John had gone beyond the line and challenged the good colonel's integrity.

This particular argument went back to 1981, when John was recording his 'Seasons of the Heart' album. As far as Milt and I were concerned, John's viability as a recording artist had gone beyond the ephemeral genres of the commercial music business. Many of his songs had by then become American standards. From a business point of view, he always made a great deal of money for RCA. Whatever he did, it was as good as gold. Let the market fluctuate. When it found its new state of equilibrium, John's work would have a place in it. On 'Seasons of the Heart,' he had done a series of love songs, including one he'd written late in the recording session at Milt's urging. It was a song he called, 'Perhaps Love:'

> *Oh, love to some is like a cloud, to some as strong as*
> *steel. For some, a way of living, for some a way to feel.*
> *And some say love is holding on, and some say letting go,*
> *and some say love is everything, and some say they don't know...*

Milt thought the song, by itself, redeemed what might otherwise be considered an abstract group on the album.

No sooner was the recording wrapped than everything went to pot. RCA decided against releasing the record, and Weintraub complied. In effect, they fired Milt, hired Larry Butler, a producer of country music, to take over, and John went to Nashville to start a new album. It was the one time I didn't join him at a recording session. He had a hard time hitting it off with Butler. It was only Milt, urging him to give it time, that kept him at it.

Milt's vanity, of course, was hurt by the firing, but he quickly dismissed it from his mind and got busy with a project for CBS Records that he had been trying to organize for a couple of years. He was producing the first recording of Placido Domingo singing contemporary material, including 'Annie's Song,' in which John played a guitar accompaniment. Milt didn't feel vindictive about what had happened. On the contrary, he was concerned that John not be put through the RCA wringer, and tried to be the voice of reason, supporting John in his strengths. This was the nurturing teacher in his character.

Butler then decided he didn't want to do *any* of John's songs. Not even 'Perhaps Love,' which has to rank among the great songs *about* love of the 20th century. That was as much an inconsiderate decision as it was stupid, and subsequent events bear this out. In the end, Butler recorded only two of the songs that John wrote for the album. Meanwhile, Milt in the midst of his work with Placido, could hardly believe this lapse of judgment, nor his good fortune. He played Placido a tape of John singing the song and Placido responded without hesitation: "John would let me record this song first? Why doesn't he record it himself?"

In fact, Milt got John to record it with Placido, and as soon as the duet was released, it received a tremendous amount of airplay. The material and the combination of voices electrified the listening public. We went to Robert Summer, the president of RCA at the time, pleading with him to co-release the duet with Columbia Records. Our feeling was that with the promotion of two major record companies, 'Perhaps Love' could become a major hit. Not only that, the wedding of Placido's operatic voice and John's contemporary voice constituted a major happening in the music world: but RCA couldn't see it. They were committed to the country album John recorded in Nashville with Butler. The 'golden' moment passed.

And so an argument with Weintraub took root. The 'Seasons of the Heart' album eventually was released by RCA and did reasonably well; it reached the charts at number 39. But it was also one of John's last recordings for RCA. In addition, Weintraub had agreed to manage Neil Diamond, who pretty much performed for the same market as John, and for all practical purposes Jerry lost sight of what he was meant to be doing with John. Also, Jerry was becoming a 'star' in his own right. His ambition to become a big-time movie producer and studio entrepreneur were crowding out his managerial obligations.

Denver didn't intend to leave the situation with Weintraub in that state of impasse. He telephoned me minutes after Weintraub,

My son, Michael and John, who together started Plant-It 2000.

almost embarrassed to say what had happened. In effect, he'd gone out to Los Angeles to fire Jerry, although what he really wanted Jerry to do was talk him out of it, and reaffirm the relationship they had had. There was a tremendous accumulation of frustration riding on it for John. He had never seen the sacker of cities so without clothes–so put upon, and out of control.

Weintraub, in that respect, reminded me of my father. Suddenly so overwhelmed with adolescent self-regard that he'd explode in a fury. But where my father would recover quickly, Weintraub became fixed in his anger, and that drew out John's anger, which he sat on. John told me that Jerry had verbally abused him and at the end of their meeting there was nothing left of the relationship to salvage.

I would have gone out and celebrated the breakup if I didn't recognize the essential sadness of what had occurred. As far as I was concerned, Jerry had reached the end of his usefulness as a manager for John. In fact, the relationship was destructive for John at that point. On the other hand, no one likes to lose a relationship that had meaning for the people involved. And nowhere does it happen with such loud reverberations as in the entertainment industry.

A few days after the blowup, as I expected, Jerry's lawyer, Bob Finkelstein, called. Weintraub was used to getting paid off when deals came unglued, and his contract with John still had two years to go. What had I to say about that? What I had to say frankly wasn't much: I thought of Marlon Brando in the film, 'Viva Zapata,' when the soldiers asked him whether he was prepared to act against authority and start the Mexican revolution. He said, "Cut the [telephone] wires!" I thought of that and suggested it was in Jerry's best interest to 'walk away!' "Walk away from the contract."

It wasn't exactly an incendiary statement, but for a few months Weintraub treated it as such. There was no *quid pro quo* that satisfied him. He was so adamant about suing if he didn't get what he felt was coming to him that I finally decided to bring in the best trial lawyers I could find. Not Los Angeles or New York 'deal men' who do brilliantly negotiating entertainment contracts. In this situation, I reached for maximum fire power and full force, the General Schwartzkopf approach, which meant attorneys who are not impressed with 'show business.' A brief they prepared, spelling out managerial transgressions that ran 14 pages, outlined the basis of a countersuit of 100 million dollars. It was like one of those gang war deals in 16th century Florence, where you went to lunch fully suited to do battle. So we, too, were armed and dangerous.

Fortunately, Jerry realized he had been hoisted by his own petard and relinquished his aggressions. I like to think something I said helped persuade him. More likely, he thought he had bigger fish to fry elsewhere. For a time, this was a man Presidents came to California to court. To see such things is to have one's faith in democratic process shaken.

Denver, of course, kept performing and recording, and doing

quite well financially, but over the course of the next dozen years his airtime on radio plummeted and that hurt. It bothered John with no letup. It bothered all of us who knew him. He cried in his beer about it, but he also tried to rise above it. It wasn't just his recording career, it was everything. It was all of his losses, public and private. But it is the public ones I can attest to.

When John was at the top, Jerry burned more than a few of his bridges for him, particularly with the folks in radio, by making John inaccessible to them. Jerry often treated radio people with contempt. He refused them interviews, and even guest seats at John's concerts. If they wanted to come to the concerts, he used to complain, let them buy tickets! That was basically Weintraub's attitude. When the peo-

Aspen, Colorado.

ple shout for bread, let them eat cake! So when John needed to draw on whatever goodwill his sociability had contrived, he found it used up.

But it wasn't in John's nature to be denied. Blocked on one path, he took a different one. As his songs fell from the charts, he gave more time to The Windstar Foundation, supporting environmental and other humanitarian actions. If his record career languished for a time, not so his fame, nor his persona. This is the period that is difficult for a lot of entertainers who have done well. They have climbed a mountain, and now they are on the other side having to climb down, and the two journeys are not equivalent. To be or not to be, that's the question.

Do you push the boulder up the hill again, or rest on your laurels?

While I was staunch among those who felt he could best serve himself and others by getting on with his development as a performing artist, I couldn't deny the nobility of his interests: world peace, a sustainable environment, the ending of human hunger. There were days, trying to get John to decide on a plan, or to agree on a concert tour that went to x, y and z, rather than a, b, and c, when I felt like Jacob wrestling with his angel. Unlike Jacob, I couldn't pin Denver to the mat.

Even if I could, I truly loved the guy and didn't want to hurt him. Instead I had to learn to co-exist with his need to work in the world in his particular way. I committed myself to trying to balance what he wanted to do with himself as a citizen of the world, which is what he was, and his career obligations. And that became the new basis of our partnership. Perhaps love, I told myself.

Oh, love to some is like a cloud, to some as strong as
steel. For some, a way of living, for some a way to feel.
And some say love is holding on, and some say letting go,
and some say love is everything, and some say they don't know...

John's descent from the mountain went through some strange and rough terrain. It took him through a second marriage full of *sturm* and *drang.* It also took him through a number of managerial arrangements, none of which seemed to last long because basically he really wanted to be his own man. For awhile, late in the game, I took on the role as his manager; I knew the business, I knew how to do it. Only I wished I had it to do 15 years earlier, because it became clear after awhile I no longer had the patience for the head games I had to play to convince John to do the things he needed to do to move his career in the right direction.

He became impatient with working on the road, and he stayed away from it for longer and longer periods. His song writing flagged, although I don't think he worked that hard at it; at least not at the level that justified his complaints. If there were glitches on the tours, he complained more than he needed. There were always glitches on the road, it's the nature of the business. There is a tension about getting a show up. Besides we had a great crew that minimized the difficulties. Complaining had just become part of John's defense mechanisms.

If the house was only three-quarters full, we had to lie to John about it. Blame it on a tornado in the next county, or a war somewhere. The sound might not be right. The venue might not be right. Perform in the Roller Dome in Holland? But, John, Placido Domingo is booked in here! The Roller Dome? He'd let you know about it a year later, when you were trying to put together yet another tour. He wasn't nasty about it, just adamant: Why do I have to do that? He felt he should sell out every show and took it somehow as a rebuke when he didn't.

On one tour to the British Isles, he called up every day with a complaint. The venues were old soccer stadiums; they'd be sold out, but he didn't care. He'd rather do a benefit at the Los Angeles Opera and make nothing than work soccer stadiums and pay his bills:

'Hal, I'm in Manchester. You can't believe the dressing room! The shower is cold!'

The next day, Phil Bowser, the detail man in Manchester would call:

'I'm calling from John's dressing room, Hal. I want you to know it's Tahiti in here.'

But again the day after that John would call; the entreaties seemed endless. He could not get it into his head that all of the people who worked for him were there partly out of love, not fear. 'If you need something,' I'd tell him, 'tell them and they will take care

of it.' In the last years, going through a second divorce, and sometimes driving after drinking, he got more demanding and less
patient. Sometimes he was plain obnoxious to people he worked
with–heads of companies–that left bad feelings. In a way he was
sinking into self-pity.

He had a thing about crying 'woe is me' in interviews which
would drive me crazy. Why would a man with $10 million appear
needy in public, a question to which he once said enigmatically, 'I'm
who I am.' I could go only so long with that attitude; I was much too
proactive to feel otherwise. There was one moment on a national television interview when he really gave into his 'woe,' and I knew he
was talking directly to me, saying in effect: Fuck you, Hal. We
laughed about it afterwards. In love and war, they say all is fair, and
at times we were in a kind of war.

On the other hand, he was a perfectionist, and what he was complaining about, at bottom, wasn't so unreasonable from his perspective. He was saying, 'Look, on stage. I'm not holding anything back.
Why shouldn't all the things that lead up to my performance be what
they are meant to be?'

What he liked best was when he could dovetail his artistic
expression with those things that he felt were his moral obligations.
He had left his church when he was a kid, but never the sense of
moral calling that went with it. A big memory for me in that regard
is Thanksgiving Day 1991 in the Big Sky country of northern
Montana. We'd come out–John and his band, the crew, the production staff, the guest artists: Clint Black, Kathy Mattea and Patty
Loveless; the director, Steve Binder–from different parts of the country to film a John Denver television Christmas Special. The exotic
location was Steve's brainchild. He proposed doing a show on the Ft.
Belnap Indian Reservation that would use the reservation and the
Assinboine and Gross Ventre tribal members who live there to create a small living tapestry of what it was, in spiritual terms, we all
return to every Christmas. As executive producer, I had the job of
convincing CBS that we knew precisely what we were doing bring-

ing crew and cast out to the west of the Badlands. CBS, thinking about its ratings, would have liked something more mainstream for the holidays: Arnold Schwarzenegger, say, singing 'Take Me Home, Country Roads' with John. Happily, we prevailed and Steve's concept proved to be a stroke of genius.

I had come in on a Sunday flight, a day after attending an interfaith concert in Harlem, at the Cathedral of St. John the Divine, in remembrance of the holocaust. The thoughts and images that the observance evoked were still with me when I landed at Great Falls, Montana; they flowed naturally in the direction we were going. At the airport, I rendezvoused with John's long-time agent at the William Morris agency, Shelly Shultz, my own Augie March, and we drove northeast for two-and-a-half hours to Chinook, 35 miles below the Canadian border, which was to be home base for the shoot. The night before, it had gone down to 20 below. Arctic air had come down from Canada. John said he'd never been so cold. I tried staying warm in my woollies.

Montana was still an abstraction in my mind more than a place on the ground. At one point, I thought I saw Buffalo Bill Cody scrambling up a hill; it couldn't be! And wasn't that a wagon train bound for California in the distance, or was I seeing things?

And by distance I mean something that defies the imagination. Wherever I looked, the sky came down around us. The dormant fields of wheat we passed went on for miles at a time. Somewhere out there, there were elk and antelope hunkering down for the long winter ahead. After a half hour, Shelly and I exhausted our wise guy repartee and fell into silence, acknowledging that out there, at least, our place in the scheme of things could be humblingly modest.

This place on the ground, I told myself, was where the morality play between the cowboys and Indians–the good guys and the bad guys–was enacted. This was what I had seen on the celluloid when I was at those Saturday morning movie programs, sitting in the darkened theater, the Bronx streets waiting to reclaim me, being confirmed in my belief that I was one of the good guys, after all. As usual, the movies had given us only a pale reflection of what there was to see and know. .

Our Badlands hosts met us and made us feel welcome. They supplied us with horses and wranglers. They were our guides. They showed us the magic of their purple-mountained majesties, whose days they live as a seamless web. In those ways, I think we all were instructed and inspired.

Our Badlands hosts us met us and made us feel welcome.

At the Cathedral of St. John the Divine, we had been asked to keep reflecting on an infamous time, so that by remembering we would avoid being doomed to repeat it. Arriving at Ft. Belnap, I couldn't help the feeling of *déjà vu*. The words uttered on Morningside Heights, overlooking the impoverished streets of central Harlem, had a prophetic resonance here, too. And I couldn't help noticing the irony of there being a town next to the reservation called Harlem, Montana. In fact, it was the only place around with a gym large enough in which John could perform. As part of our filming and as a token of appreciation and acknowledgment of the tribes, John performed two shows for the two thousand Indian families in the area. No one of note had ever come there and done that before.

Harlem, Montana, had fared no better in the economic struggle than Harlem, New York. On the reservation, unemployment was almost 80 percent. But it was a tribal reality; no one went hungry because of it; no one was without shelter. Deprived and neglected, they were still a proud and courageous people sharing on their native ground.

Nowhere did that fact come home to me more forcefully than when our guides took us into deep country to see their buffalo herd. When it had become legal again to do, they had assembled a herd of 15; now that herd numbered about 100. Up close, I could see why these large creatures were treasured by the tribes on the plains. One of those magnificent beasts can feed 1,200 people at one time.

Each day we were there, we were taken in hand and led into another dimension of the place. What on arriving seemed undifferentiated terrain began to reveal its particularities. Our friends guided us to hidden caves, majestic buttes, wonderful walking trails. On the level of historical consciousness, I don't know if I'd ever dug down so deeply into my ancestral roots as an American.

It was a week bracketed with haunting reminders of debts we all have in the here and now. It conjured up feelings I still hadn't worked through. My mother had died earlier in the year. And my daughter Amy had just miraculously survived a near-fatal car accident. Reflecting on those things made me realize I was still, in a sense, on edge, holding back breath. For that miracle, out there on the prairie. I gave thanks again, and felt the smallest muscles in my body release the tension.

This was life on the road at its most spartan. But the sheer fortitude that was required of everybody seemed to bring us closer together. When I say a team spirit evolved, I mean it in its most basic sense. Our work took on a spiritual dimension. And to the logistician in me most amazing was the fact that despite the bitter cold and snow, all 80 members of the production team made it on the days they were supposed to arrive. Did we do that to the prairie or did the prairie do that to us?

At the end of filming, the Assinboine and Gross Ventre recognized the special efforts of cast and crew and gave them gifts as their tradition demands. On Thanksgiving Day, the light disappearing in the west, and the place itself haunted by spirits, we filmed Thanksgiving dinner with the tribal council, our guides, John, his guest artists. The tribes had volunteered to prepare the meal: roast turkey, breaded stuffing with apples and raisins, cranberry sauce, creamed onions, sweet peas, acorn squash. At tables just behind the cameras, the staff and crew joined in. For the television special, we called it Christmas dinner. On some deep level of remembering, it became for me the first Thanksgiving.

10

Turning the Corner

Missing man formation.

The phone call telling us about John's death registered like a clap of thunder. It is still registering, years later. Thunder, and then lightning where I stood. For the length of a long breath, as I was told the story, it felt like a part of me had died as well. Doe and I had already been asleep–we were in New York, where it was past the witching hour–so I was more than a little disarmed and disoriented hearing the story.

The sheriff's office in Monterey had found pieces of John's plane–a home-built fiberglass two-seater that he had bought only a few days earlier–floating on the surface of Monterey Bay near where a plane had crashed earlier that afternoon. They'd also found his car parked at the airport outside of Carmel. The crash had left whoever was flying the plane so broken up that it was hard to be sure about identification. They wanted to know if I had spoken to John that day; if I knew where else he might be? If someone else had taken his plane up, driven his car? My mind raced over all the possibilities, but

I knew it was just an exercise in grasping at straws.

One moment the plane seemed to be operating normally, according to witnesses, and the next in a nose dive from which it never recovered. Witnesses said the impact of the crash reverberated across the bay. There was lots of conjecturing about it later: A bird had got drawn into the front assembly, jamming the engine! The fuel had run out in one tank and there was nothing in reserve! John, in his instinctive response to danger, must have touched the wrong control!

Whatever happened, in that moment of reversal, positive to negative, it remains somewhat of a mystery. None of the conjectures make any sense to me. John was an excellent pilot, well-schooled and experienced. He flew light planes, jets and even gliders. Whatever happened–and we may never know–my heart and head tell me that pilot error was not part of the process.

In my reveries about him, I see him just before the moment of impact, trying to be the person he thought he needed to be, whoever that was, doing what he thought needed to be done. John had that kind of resolve. Once skiing downhill on one of the wilderness runs outside of Aspen, he got caught in an avalanche that might have killed him right then. For a minute or two, he couldn't be seen, and it was hard to imagine him, or anyone, coming out of that cascade of packed snow unharmed. And then, there he was, still upright, knees tucked, looking straight ahead, showing no alarm, certainly no fear, coming along as if nothing was happening, coming home at the bottom of the hill. He never gave an inch to it, fighting it off all the way down.

It's not much consolation, but I like to think that he enjoyed that last hour of flight as much as anything he'd ever experienced. The year before, I might have thought otherwise. For the better part of 10 years, there weren't many big stretches of time when he wasn't struggling with himself about something. What it was about, on any given day, I'm not sure I could say. There was so much: himself; things that haunted him. His marriages, his wives. The loss of his father. There were so many issues, public and private, that pushed and pulled at him. They seemed to come at him all at once.

Ironically, in the months before the crash, he seemed to get free of whatever was taking him down. You could hear him saying so, in so many ways. He had just finished doing a series of concerts with various symphonies. We were putting together a new tour. He was working with Milt Okun on an album of covers, which were songs he wished he had written. He wanted to do it for years, and kept putting it off. He was moving on to another level of relationship with his children. Zach and Anna Kate were young adults, and Jessie Belle was growing up. He wanted not to take their love and respect for granted. It was like a man returning from the proverbial seven years of wandering in the wilderness, and discovering that he had a life to live.

Part of it, too, was being able to put a second divorce behind him. That included difficult, and extended, divorce proceedings which tore him up emotionally (it almost tore me up, for different reasons). Where I grew up, nothing seemed more sorrow-laden than the breakdown of a marriage, except maybe death. Fear of it, in regard to my own parent's marriage, shadowed me all the time I was growing up. I watched John go through it twice; each time, emotionally in it with him, up to my ears.

Fortunately when Annie sued for divorce, it was almost like a bank transfer. Both sides were in basic agreement about what needed to be done, and they let me be the arbiter of what was fair. Still John suffered the ignominy of the divorce for a long time. Much as he wanted out of the marriage, he never stopped loving Annie. And after their resentments toward each other faded or were talked out, Annie and he became best friends, which meant a great deal to John.

The real key to his turning the corner, I think, was what he worked out with his soul finally about who he would be. It is slightly ironic that John suffered so over that question because, in important ways, there is no one I know who was more his own man, and more fearless in being so. But he had a hangup: he was overattached to the child he was; and still waiting for some sign of recognition.

Which is a hard fantasy to apprehend.

Out of curiosity once, I had asked John what name his father called him by: his given name was Henry John, same as his dad's. This was a good 10 years after his father had died. Had Dutch called him John or Henry, or what? His mood stiffened suddenly, and his eyes filled with emotion. Finally, he said: "My dad never called me anything, except: 'Hey! Boy!'"

Dorothy in 1998, ageless.

Why Dutch never acknowledged to John, boy and man—to whom he was a monumental figure, an air ace and, in his own way, a man of conscience—why Dutch never acknowledged whatever it was that John felt he needed to hear from him, I don't know. That was something left unresolved between them: father-and-son relationships hide all sorts of intensities. Over time, they give way. Dutch had been a tough taskmaster and while he mellowed as he grew older he never let up on teasing John about his celebrity. He wouldn't be impressed, he once told John, until John had been invited to play in the Celebrity Golf Tournament at Pebble Beach, which is of course what finally happened.

I find it very poignant that when John died he was practicing a routine of landings and takeoffs that his father had taught him. He was trying to get the plane down, and up, in the way Dutch would have approved. How much further can you carry filial piety?

In fact, as a family man, John was like a throwback to his dad, as if in some chauvinist act of homage. John and I used to kid a lot about how our respective fathers took charge of the show when they came home from their labors. When Dutch came home, he wanted

With Annie Denver.

the food on the table and everybody to obey orders. John was gentler, but his behavior was still a variation on that theme. He came into the marriage with Annie with a lot of assumptions that were undeveloped, and he never changed them.

At the height of his recording success, he'd be on the road for months at a time, and had really stopped sharing an outside life with her. I don't remember him staying home ever. And when Annie showed herself to be an independent person, making a life for herself when he wasn't around, cultivating friends he couldn't or wouldn't share, and she persisted in those friendships, he felt threatened by that.

John's second marriage, to Cassandra Delaney, an Australian singer, developed in exactly the opposite direction, a strange irony that. Cassie was much younger than John, and in general a "party girl." She and her Aspen friends wanted to be out every night playing. John, on the other hand, wanted more of a sedate home life when he returned from touring. It was not marriage-made-in-heaven, but then which marriages are?

In the end I think he just decided to stop lacerating himself over what had gone wrong. I think he saw how he could make things work for himself again. I think he was reaching down into his spiri-

Aspen Snowmass Jazz festival.

tual resources, reorganizing himself. His spiritual resourcefulness accounted for a lot of the positive things people felt about him wherever he went in the world. People recognized him as having real commitments to the human side of the equation; they knew that about him, and that he was one of them, whether *they* were the Russians, the Chinese, the Irish, the Dutch; whoever.

After we went to China, John wrestled with his career but halfheartedly. He couldn't be reconciled with not being at the top in his field. His lamenting about it was constant: "It's one thing to climb a mountain, another to get down." By the early 1990s, his music had virtually disappeared from the airwaves. He was still an enormously popular figure as a performer, but for a long time his recording success was in eclipse and he had little interest in exploring other 'uses' of his popularity, except those that played into his social concerns. I wanted him to explore other areas of the entertainment industry that were open to him. When I got my feet wet as a theatrical producer, I urged John to come in alongside me.

Pierre Cossette had the idea of doing a musical revue based on the life of Will Rogers and sought out John to play Will and write the score. John was in fact the inspiration for Cossette's project. Denver and Rogers shared an uncanny resemblance, both as public entertainers and as 'citizens at large.' They even shared cultural roots in the hardscrabble of Oklahoma. Both were pilots. (Both died in plane crashes.) But the truth is John didn't want to work that hard anymore. He certainly didn't want to be spending months in New York working on that project. The road had become an ordeal.

On stage, his sense of showmanship was as masterful as ever, his voice better than ever. But backstage, after a show, or before the show, he'd groan and moan as a way of communicating his frustrations. Plus he'd met Cassandra, and his life became a series of alternating currents made up of love, loss, and reconciliations. Nothing was simple for him anymore, not even love. Especially love.

Within that labor of emotionally scaling back from being number one, there'd be long periods when, instead of going on the road or going into the recording studio and working, John chose to roam the world, a world he had made familiar to himself more than most people get to do. But always he loved coming home, and Aspen was home. Or more specifically the place he and Annie had built, set into the brow of a hill on Starwood mountain. It was his eagle's aerie.

Only this last time, instead of coming home, John's ashes had to be brought home, a task that fell to John's close friends, Jerry

Jampolsky and his wife, Diane Cirrincione, creators of the world-wide Centers for Attitudinal Healing. They lived up the coast from where John was killed, and made of their accompaniment of John's ashes a spiritual crossing. At the funeral, in Aurora, John's remains were buried beside his father's, and we eulogized him: a son, a brother, a father and a friend, who had also been an icon for an age.

As one of the eulogists I tried to bring closure to what I was feeling, but managed only to dent the surface of it. The image of the Air Force Thunderbirds that flew overhead in a 'missing man' formation when John's dad had been buried, came into my thoughts, except I saw myself at the controls of one of the planes. In some ways, I'm still there, still trying to keep my end of the formation straight, still moving in that direction. In Aspen there's now a John Denver sanctuary on Roaring Fork River, which invites people to come for quiet reflection, and be reminded of the man and his music, and the way he held himself as a steward of the earth. And then in 2002 there'll be a theater production based on John's music that will provide a new outlet for the songs that still mean so much to so many people. After that, who knows? For now, I'm in a time bend, to use Arthur Miller's phrase; I'm traveling my life lines. In one direction I'm going forward along roads being laid down by the new millennium; in the other, I'm somewhat compulsively drawn back to the place from where I've come, making sure I've covered my bets.

*

From Bordeaux to the Dordogne it is a three-hour car trip, full of gastronomic enticements. Each town and village you drive through has at least a half dozen places you want to stop at–for *un café, une baguette, un chocolat,* some cheese, a glass of wine, a *soufflé.* It's my hidden epicurean self rattling its chains. (As someone whose epicurean roots are in hot dogs with mustard and sauerkraut, it doesn't take much to get me going.) I'm trying to get to where John Malkovich and his family are staying before dark.

When Malkovich left the "True West" company to pursue a film career, nearly 20 years ago, we decided to keep working together as financial counselor and client, and a number of times a year, almost ritualistically, we meet to review the pragmatics (financial statements). Since Malkovich has moved with Nicole Peyran and their children to the Luberon valley in the south of France, our little seminars have taken a certain continental turn. Sometimes we covene in the village where Malkovich lives (which has a *pissoir* on its public square that almost puts modern civilization to shame); other times, on location, where he is doing a film. Often–which adds to it for me–it is in the context of family life. That allows me to catch different dimensions of the man, and to see him growing into himself, which makes what I do more real. It is how it worked with Denver. For me, a student of the entertainment industry in all its manifestations, these moments on the road are great occasions.

I remember how CCNY, by way of motivation, used to dangle before us the notion that there were 'world's to conquer' and that if we paid attention to the basics that they were imparting to us, we'd be in on it. It was meant as a figure of speech, but we took it as a mantra–repeating it to ourselves *sotto voce* on the subway to and from classes, and on the corner at night, standing there, waiting for Godot. It was the one portentousness we allowed ourselves. But ordinary colonialists we weren't. It was part of our conceit (and a matter of pride) to feel that wherever we ended up as conquerors we would come down on the side of our angels. To me that meant keeping faith with my father's dreams as much as my own. It feels that way still.

Give or take a year, it is half a century since I worked with my father; since I stood behind the counter of his deli, the man in charge of closing up, doling out late-night containers of coffee to whoever wandered in from Third Avenue, and frustrated every minute I was standing there that I couldn't figure out how to keep the family business from dying. In fifty years, a lot has changed for me. But the impulse to make things happen, whether for myself or for a client, persists.

For months, for example, Malkovich had an idea about putting some of his money to work in a restaurant and disco complex on the waterfront in Lisbon. Friends of his in the barrio Alto own a restaurant called Papasorda's, and want him to go in with them in a new place they're opening in the harbor area. Having once been a partner in a syndicate that operated Sardi's, on Shubert's Alley in New York, I can understand the interest, and I relish the symmetry. Am I being dreamy in my impulse to buy in, or acting soundly? Letting my passion get the better of me, or being smart? Would I help him figure it out. (And if it is smart to do, I might come in on it myself.

On set of Shadow of the Vampire, 1998.

Partnering, I find, automatically enlivens the action for me–even when the partnership is operating mainly on spiritual capital.)

For actors and entertainers, life is a balancing act. They have to balance time for family with time for work and time for themselves. My job, said simply, is to insulate them from the vagaries of their business and get them to where there is enough income working for them so that they don't have to take jobs that demean their talent, or that pulls them away from their focus. Without focus their gifts are wasted.

Fittingly, the last day of my visit, a tour of the local sights, took John, Nicole, their children and myself to Les Milandes, Josephine Baker's family chateau: the product of a balancing act par excellence. Baker's legend, of course, preceded me to the Bronx. It was part of schoolboy lore there (besides sheltering us in a bubble of obscurity, the Bronx of the Forties and Fifties was a haven for modernist enthusiasms). But what we knew about her (international celebrity at the age of 19, self-exiled in France, the toast of Paris) was all drawn from the Broadway gossip columns which, along with the baseball and football scores, were standard reading fare for us. About the real story, we knew next to nothing.

In the enduring myth, Baker made it on her own: on her own talent and on her own terms. In real life, the story was more complex and richer. Two years after she triumphed in La Revue négre, she

Josephine Baker with US troops, WWII.

announced her marriage to a Roman count. The marriage was actually a liaison with a Sicilian gigolo. But the 'count' protected her money, shaped her career and endured her affairs. By his death a decade later, Josephine had not only metamorphed into Joséphine, the empress of entertainment, she was allegedly the most highly paid performer in Europe. Though I would hesitate to compare myself to a gigolo, its a story that reverberates for me. Certainly the theme repeats itself endlessly in show business lives. Why this need be the case more than in other fields (or maybe it isn't) beats me.

Mulling over this and other cunundrum, as the old codgers on the block used to say, and watching the Mistral kick up, I bid Malkovich and his family adieu, reset my watch, and retrace the route that brought me from the airport in Bordeaux the previous day. Taking in the sights, the sounds and the culinary temptations from a reverse angle for the three hours it takes again, lets me fantasize about them all over again but differently. That night, at Papasorda's in Lisbon, John's friends regale me with their grandiose visions of things to come. Before dinner is over, we've become complicit; my being from the Bronx, interestingly, gives me a certain caché, as if what was once obscuring is now to be celebrated–and for my part I'm thrilled to meet true Lisbonese. If I like what I see, they say, then the question is how much to go in for? What to go in for is always the $64 question! The situation seems to call for the pioneering spirit.

My textbook take on 'the pioneering spirit' was shaped in seventh grade. In the assigned texts, 'the pioneering spirit' was represented by a tableaux showing a dour group of Puritans, dressed in the garments of 'our forebears' (that's what the book said), making their way into the wilderness. (I think this is how it had stood in my head all these years. In one part of my head there was the Puritan fathers and in another part was Josephine Baker.) In Lisbon, looking out over the Atlantic toward New York, I finally connect with the gravity of being a pioneer. But rather than being an onerous proposition, the pioneering spirit fills me with a bouyancy that feels lighter than air.

In the end, you leave a place but you take some part of it with you: the tastes, for one thing; the sounds, for another. The views from the hills; all the possibilities of what's new and novel...

ENCORE

Before I knew how I wanted to live, even before I had found anything remotely approaching direction or purpose, or an understanding of where in the greater scheme of things we belonged and how it mattered; before the Superbowl, three-point plays, designated hitters, instant replay; before either corporate America or Aquarian Age metaphysics took hold; before Elvis, Clinton, Bush, Carter, Reagan, Ford, Nixon, Kennedy and

At the National Arts Club, on Gramercy Park in Manhattan, March 2001, following a reading by Cliff Robertson of his play at Food for Thought, a new producing venture. To the right of Robertson are Susan Charlotte and Barry Minsky, two of my co-producers, and Aldon James, president of the club.

Eisenhower, there was just us: this group of pint-sized public school boys by day, learning the basics of the American credo as FDR's New Deal defined it, and the last of the New York Indians (as my mother would call us) by night, standing obscurely at a corner of a crossroads in the East Bronx, like birds on a wire.

We moved to Aspen for good about 10 years ago. We had been coming for one thing and another for years, staying for longer and longer periods. Finally we upped the ante, traded in the condo, and found a real house. We moved our furniture in, we hung our paintings , and last year we got a dog: a large waif–half wolf, half labrador from the looks of him–left at the local pound abandoned. Over time we've threaded ourselves into a new circle of friendships; the circle has expanded into a 'crowd'–one of the many that contribute to "the life" as Aspen knows it. Dorothy, who has always been a community activist in the mantle of wise woman, has made me over into an activist in her image: full-hearted, sober, civic-minded. She tells me to think of it–and I do–as a process of personal growth.

Being part of a crowd still defining itself, as opposed to one inherited and all sorted out, is a singular experience. It's also a peculiarly accomplished crowd–both in its constituent parts and its totality. Nearly everyone has their own Horatio Alger stories going, their own pipe dreams working. They manage to remain loyal to the principle of the social contract writ locally yet they march to their own drummer. Every year, for weeks and months at a time, the crowd disperses attending to their individual itineraries. Adventures of one sort or another lay claim to everyone's time. It is not your traditional retirement village, but people are free to travel and do. Then, when the bungee cords that tie people to Aspen reach the ends of their give–it has something to do with the phases of the moon, the alignment of the stars–the crowd returns, delighted to be in each other's company again. There is no actual candy store there helping me feel anchored, but what's there stands in for the candy store. As I cycle or drive to one or another of our rendezvous points, I'm conscious of the historical resonances.

In my youth, Fridays were the best days of the week, and Friday night was the icing on the cake. Anyone who had been a New York Indian from that time and place will tell you as much. It meant no more 'school' until Monday. It meant being out from under the thumb of authority. And, for our particular community, it meant being covered over with a veil of spiritual transcendence, which you breathed in and breathed out, observant or not; whether your thoughts were pure or bent. Somehow the community, as community, made a space that was sacrosanct, and you were part of it. You were imbued with its spirit, and with a sense of worth. It was a great gift, and whose call I'm still susceptible to.

What I miss about New York away from it, out of town, *pace* Billy Strayhorn's idea that when you're out of Manhattan you are "out-of-town," is the throb and the beat: *le tom de coeur*, as the French say. Although Aspen, in its own way, is a cultural mecca, there is nothing in it that can replace New York's cultural diversity: the give and take; the push and pull; the sense of democratic striving, which underwrites it all.

It is meaningful to me too, still, being able to casually press the flesh with my original co-conspirators, the last of the New York Indians with whom I continue to be in touch. Though now we juggle different sets of experiences and values, in addition to what we started with, there is something soulful (even hilarious–although hilarity might not to be the note I'm after) about this abiding involvement. Our long adolescent ardor for each other, and the pratfalls we shared, have sealed us in a place where time waits. Each re-meeting, however fleeting, is a small epiphany: beyond commentary or category. It is not the sort of thing you enshrine in a pantheon–which would be like trying to apprehend a rainbow, but the aura we create together informs everything.

The oddest thing of all is how, standing or sitting together in a public place, the mantle of obscurity returns. The other day a tour bus passed us, while we were sitting on a bench on Third Avenue, having our decaf lattés, and we could hear ourselves being 'narratized' by the tour guide for the sake of the tour. We were cast as romantic figures: low-life denizens of a changing neighborhood–as an ensemble, we have that look.

After John's death, I tried to negotiate a deal with a young singer-and-songwriter who was making a name for herself in Colorado. I began imagining myself going out 'on the road' again. (They've found that when you lose a limb, you continue to feel it.). Could I get back into it? With a new face? Not only a new face, in fact, but a new generation? I went to a couple of performances and saw flashes of Janis Joplin and Billie Holiday. What a parley, I thought. I met with the mom, who was managing this talent, and talked career development. She had booked her daughter into gigs at a couple of clubs in New York, two of the newer venues, and I came in for it. It was, as Yogi Berra said, *déjà vu* all over again.

Except that it wasn't a scene that physically I was too familiar with. Sitting at tables seems to have become *passé*. The young now simply stand in front of the band stand and groove. Personal growth hasn't brought me there yet. But I loved the show: I was imagining all sorts of scenarios for creating show business magic. Unfortunately, the possibilities didn't fall the way I was envisioning them. Ebb and flow go with the territory.

I'm still driving myself to accomplish goals; I still feel the need to make more of things. I still run after chimeras, I still haven't had enough. Dorothy wants to know if I know what enough is.

The mountains may be enough. Most of the time they are more than enough. For one thing there are more than 300 days in the year when the sun shines down. Those like myself who are still reaching for the golden ring, wheel and counter wheel in this luminous setting, but the degree of hubris, which is always in play, is kept in check. Moguls, working people, and ski bums crowd the ski slopes together, but all on the same level. The most important attribute at that time is how good you look on skiis and how well you navigate the moguls on the slopes.

As the guys in public relations are wont to say, it is god's country—essentially. And within that, it is a place still where Friday night comes, with its veil of transcendence, which I find life-affirming, metaphorically if not metaphysically. The simple set of command- ments that I learned to live with many years ago still order my moral universe. Now that my two children are grown, I can lay claim to a fresh understanding of those tenets, having watched how both of them, as they matured, embody their meaning. For even obscurity has texture, which time, and the gifts of friendship, allow you to explore.

What the Poet Laureate, Robert Pinsky, wrote comes to mind:

For place, itself, is always a kind of motion,
A part of it artificial and preserved,
And a part born in a blur of loss and change
All places in motion from where we thought they were,
Boston before it was Irish or Italian,
Harlem and Long Branch before we ever knew
That they were beautiful, and when they were:
Our nation, mellowing to another country
Of different people living in different places.

The Bronx and Broadway: two places that make a whole for me. A kind of motion, a blur of loss and change.

In the meantime, on with the show.

***